miss O™ & friends

CAUGHT IN THE 'NET

CAUGHT IN THE 'NET

By Juliette, with
Devra Newberger Speregen

Illustrated by Hermine Brindak

Watson-Guptill Publications/New York

For Jordan, one truly cool dude.

Senior Editor: Julie Mazur
Editor: Cathy Hennessy
Production Manager: Katherine Happ

First published in 2006 by Watson-Guptill Publications, a division of VNU Business Media, Inc.,
770 Broadway, New York, NY 10003
www.watsonguptill.com

Library of Congress Cataloging-in-Publication Data

Speregen, Devra Newberger.
Miss O & friends : caught in the 'net / by Juliette, with Devra Newberger Speregen ; illustrated by Hermine Brindak.
p. cm.
Summary: With help from her sister, Miss O, and their friends, Juliette creates an online 'zine for school which becomes an instant hit, but as the emails pour in, Juliette wonders how to juggle the work while trying to identify who is sending her funny and smart anonymous emails.
ISBN-13: 978-0-8230-2948-8 (alk. paper)
ISBN-10: 0-8230-2948-4 (alk. paper)
[1. Journalism—Fiction. 2. Schools—Fiction. 3. Best friends—Fiction. 4. Friendship—Fiction.] I. Brindak, Hermine, ill. II. Title. III. Title: Miss O and friends. IV. Title: Caught in the 'net.
PZ7.S7489Mir 2006
[Fic]—dc22

2006021652

Printed in the U.S.A.

First printing 2006

Contents

Meet the group!

Welcome to Miss O and Friends!

When I, the real Juliette, was ten years old, I created the basis for Miss O and Friends. It all started when I was on the way home from a family vacation. I was bored, so I tried to think of something fun to do. The only thing that I could really do was draw. I borrowed some paper from my mom and started to draw "cool girls." I gave them to my mom and, like all mothers, she told me they were nice and put them in her purse. Little did she know that one day these drawings would turn into something much bigger.

Years later, with the help of my mom, my sister, and some friends, we started to create the Miss O girls. At first, it was just something fun to do—we'd play around on the computer creating all sorts of stuff. It wasn't until we realized that girls really liked our characters that the idea came to us to start a company. Now, thanks to girls like you, the Miss O and Friends Web site (www.missoandfriends.com) has become the most popular tween site ever!

The five Miss O girls are based on girls just like you and me, and they all possess important values and do things they love to do. This series of books features a story from each of the girls. In this book, Juliette (who's based on me!) tells her story. I hope you enjoy it!

Chapter 1

Keeping Cool Back at School

"Your vacation sounds totally awesome, Harlie!" I told one of my best friends as I moved around her to hang a brand-new mirror on the inside of my locker. I held the small mirror against the inside of the door and looked at her for approval.

"Straight?" I asked.

Harlie blew her dark black bangs from her eyes and nodded. "Yup! Looks good, Juliette!"

My sister, Olivia, then reached around me and put a sticker over the mirror. It was a big, pink, glittery sticker and it said: *A Princess Lives Here*. When I read it, I totally cracked up! So did Harlie, and Justine, and Isabella (my other two BFFs.) We laughed because everyone knows how much I hate the whole "princessy, pink, glittery" look.

It's just *so* not me.

"Take that off, Miss O!" I cried. I call my sister "Miss O," which is short for "Olivia." Actually, *everyone* calls her Miss O. My father gave her that nickname when she was little because he said it fit her sassy personality. Since then, it has stuck.

Miss O happily peeled the sticker off the locker and crumpled it up. "Just kidding, Juliette!" she said with a smile.

"We know how much you *love* pink," Isabella said sarcastically. Then she yawned. "Gosh, it's early," she mumbled. "Feels weird being at school so early." Isabella pushed a bright orange headband back over her long, brown hair. Having just returned from a two-week trip to Peru to visit with her mother's family, Izzy looked great. The bright orange headband really stood out next to her sun-kissed skin.

"Early?" Harlie said with a laugh. "This is nothing! I get up much earlier than this every morning for gymnastics training. And anyway, I love getting to school before all the other kids. These empty halls are perfect for wheely-ing!" Harlie spun on her heels and began to "wheely" down the hall. Harlie's "Wheelys" were her newest obsession. They'd been a gift to her from her parents for the Chinese New Year last week (Harlie's family is Chinese and the Chinese New Year is a *huge* deal in her family). She's worn them every day since!

"Don't forget to take out the wheels on those when school starts," Justine reminded her. "If a teacher sees you wearing those in school, you'll get in trouble—big time!"

Harlie nodded as she wheeled past us. "I know, I know," she said.

"Are you excited about second term?" Justine asked me as she helped Miss O arrange my little bottles of hair care products on the top shelf of my locker.

In case you were wondering why my best friends and my sister and I were in school on a Monday morning so early, it was because they were all helping me decorate my locker with all the funky cool stuff I bought in New York City over winter break.

The five of us attend the Sage School in Westchester, New York. Sage is a private school with three divisions: lower, middle, and upper. I'm the oldest and I'm in my first year of middle division. (That's like sixth grade in public school.) Miss O and the other girls are all in last year lower division (fifth grade).

Anyway, every year we have a three-week break that starts with the holidays in December and runs into January. It's awesome because it's a really long vacation! During this year's break, my family went on a few short trips, rather than one long one. We went to Washington, D.C., and then to Boston, Massachusetts, for a few days, which was so, so fun! Oh, and we went skiing in upstate New York at Windham Mountain, too. Miss O and I went to "ski school": both got pretty good! And during the last week of winter break, Mom, Dad, Miss O, and I went on a big shopping and sightseeing day in New York City. That was the best!

On a walk through New York City's Greenwich Village, Miss O and I found the funkiest little store. They had so many cool things inside that I was inspired to redecorate my school locker. I practically wiped out my entire savings in that store alone! I found tons of locker-type things all in periwinkle blue (my most fave color!) like a locker mirror, a dry-erase board in the shape of a microphone, and a dozen daisy-shaped magnetic hooks for hanging stuff. I especially love the hooks, because now I have a place to hang all my spare hair ties and necklaces that I keep in my locker for fashion emergencies.

I thought about Justine's question: *Was* I excited about the second term starting? Then I yawned. (It really was early! Too early to be in school, anyway.) But I was anxious to start the new term, especially because I was

about to begin a new class this term: Computer Clicks. I had managed to snag a spot in the popular class for first period every morning. I was so stoked! Mr. Adams, who teaches the class, is the best, most interesting teacher in school. I heard he used to be a journalist, too, which was why I *really* wanted to be in his class. I would love to become a journalist some day! That's one of my dreams, anyway.

So I nodded. "Yeah, second term is gonna rock," I told her.

"You're so lucky," Justine remarked as she began attaching magnetic photo clips (yes, periwinkle clips!) all over the inside of my locker door. "I heard Computer Clicks is such a fun class! You get to design web pages and create blogs and stuff. I would love to learn all that. My friend in London started her own blog," Justine went on. "It's just like an online journal, so I can log onto my computer at home and read all about what's going on in her life."

If you're wondering why Justine has close friends in London, it's because she used to live there before she moved to Westchester. Justine's father was a general in the United States Army and her family had lived in many places all over the world. Luckily, her father retired last year and they haven't had to move again. I don't know what I'd do if Justine had to move away!

"Check this out!" Justine said. "I have a present for you! It's a new picture of us to hang up in your locker! So you'll think about us poor lower division souls while you're living it up in middle division all day!"

Justine clipped the photograph to the locker door and I leaned in to take a look. It was a picture of the five of us that her mother had taken right before winter break, at the big school carnival. I had to laugh when I saw it—in the photo, all five of us were totally cracking up!

Looking at the photo over my shoulder, Isabella started laughing. "That was the funniest day of my life!" she exclaimed. "Look at me in that picture! I was laughing so hard that my face was bright red!"

"That *was* hysterical," Miss O agreed with a chuckle. "I laughed so hard I almost . . . well, *you know*!"

"*Eeew!*" Isabella squealed.

"Well it's true!" Miss O said! "I had just finished two whole extra-large lemonades! I had to cross my legs together so nothing would, you know, come out!"

Justine laughed and rolled her eyes. "Yuck! You are *so* gross!"

I laughed, remembering the carnival and why we'd been laughing so hard that day. Miss O's teacher—Mrs. Hintermeister—had just been dunked in the dunk tank! It was so funny to see the strictest teacher in the school fall into the water with all her clothes on!

"Oh, and remember how I snorted really loudly from laughing so hard?" Harlie chimed in as she wheeled on by.

"How could we forget?" I called out to her. "It was right in front of all those cute upper division boys!"

Harlie bit her bottom lip and grinned sheepishly. "Right. Sorry about that!" she said.

"I think they were laughing just as hard as we were at the Hinter Monster," Miss O pointed out. "So they probably never even noticed your snort."

"Well, thanks for the picture, Justine," I told her. "I really love it. Just seeing it is going to put me in a good mood!"

By the way, you should know I *also* love that picture because I look

really good in it! Well, I don't mean to sound all conceited or anything, but I *was* having an *excellent* hair day. I usually *hate* how I look in pictures, but that morning I had used a new leave-in conditioner and it had made my hair look really great.

"C'mon, Juliette! You just like how your hair looked that day!" Miss O commented as she squeezed past me to reach into the locker and stick up another periwinkle hook.

I gave her a playful shove. "Ha, ha," I said. "So what if I do?"

As I reached across my sister to put up another daisy hook, a strange voice spoke behind me.

"That picture was from the carnival, right?" the voice said.

I spun around to find myself face to face with a very cute boy in my grade, Noah Sclar. It totally startled me for two reasons: First, because I had thought that we were the only kids in the building at this early hour, and second, because Noah Sclar was incredibly popular at school and had never said a word to me before.

"Oh! Hi! Um, yes. It was," I replied. "At the carnival. It was, um, taken at the carnival. The picture, I mean." *Oh, brother. What was wrong with me? Why couldn't I get out a coherent sentence?*

"That carnival was a blast," Noah said with a laugh. "Remember when the Hinter Monster got dunked?" Noah's eyes sparkled when he smiled. And his brown curls were almost as bouncy as Justine's—every time he moved, they bounced in different directions. OMG, he was *so* cute!

"Yeah!" I said with a grin. "That was hilarious. My sister has the Hinter Monster, you know."

"Hi," Miss O said. "I'm Juliette's sister, Olivia. Everyone calls me Miss O."

"Hey," Noah said to her. "Cool. Who is Juliette?" he asked.

I felt my face turn red. "*I'm* Juliette," I said. "We're in the same grade."

"Really?" Noah asked blankly.

I nodded. "But we've never had class together. Oh, um, these are my friends Justine, Isabella, and Harlie. They're all in lower division with Miss O."

"*Last year* lower division," Harlie pointed out, trying to sound as mature as possible.

"Cool," Noah said again. He stared at me. "I've seen you before, but I didn't know your name. Now I do."

Just as he spoke, a loud version of Green Day's "Good Riddance" (FYI—fave song alert!) sounded from my locker.

"Huh—?" Noah asked, startled by the music echoing in the locker.

I pulled my brand-new cell phone out from its new periwinkle locker cell phone holder. "Ring tone," I explained. "It's a text message."

"You have your own cell?" he asked. "Sweet."

I couldn't help but smile, suddenly feeling *very* hip. "Yeah," I said coolly. "My parents got it for me over break."

I gazed down at the text message that, unfortunately, Noah was reading over my shoulder. It said: **key n mlbx. LUV U, DADDY**

I felt myself blush. Just perfect . . . my first text message ever, being read over my shoulder by the cutest boy ever . . . *and it was from my father!*

And he'd called himself "Daddy!"

"Who's it from, Juliette?" Miss O asked.

I cleared my throat in embarrassment. "Uh, it's from Dad," I told her quietly. "He's, um, leaving the house key in the mailbox." I felt myself blush again, having to talk about dorky stuff like parents and house keys in front of Noah.

Fortunately, Noah didn't seem to mind at all.

"Juliette's parents are the best," Isabella told him. "And her father is a musician. He plays in a rock band and everything!"

Noah's eyes widened. "Yeah?" he asked me.

I nodded. "Yes," I explained, "but they play mostly eighties music like Bruce Springsteen. Stuff like that."

"Still, that's pretty excellent," Noah said. "I'm in a band, too, you know."

Did I know? Did I know?

Ha!

Of course I knew that Noah was in a band! Every girl at Sage knew Noah Sclar was the lead singer and guitarist for As If!

"Um, yeah. You play in As If, right?" I tried to sound as casual as I could.

Noah grinned. *There were those bright eyes again!* "Yup. And we've got some totally new tunes for this year's Sage Sings show," he added. "You should come check us out sometime. We play Green Day and other awesome stuff."

I could *feel* the girls staring at the back of my head as I smiled and nodded to Noah. "Maybe I will," I said. "Sounds fun."

Miss O secretly nudged me from behind. "*Sounds fun!*" she whispered, in an effort to mimic me.

I spun around and shot her a look.

At that same moment, I realized the halls were beginning to get busier. Other students had begun arriving at school, and the sound of lockers being opened and slammed shut were all around us. I suddenly felt a pang of excitement in my stomach, thinking that second term was just minutes away!

Unlike a lot of other kids I know, I was actually *glad* for school to start up again. Mostly because I was taking three brand-new classes this term, two of which were creative writing classes. I've loved writing ever since I could hold a pen. My mom tells me I used to write all sorts of crazy stuff when I was little, like family newspapers and even dinner menus! It's still a family joke whenever we have "olives" at our house. We call them "I Loves" because that's what I thought they were called when I was little, and that's what I called them on my first ever family menu: *I loves . . . 3 cents each.*

"Juliette," Miss O said, interrupting the memory, "it's almost time for the bell. We'd better head over to the lower division building."

I gave my sister a hug. "Okay," I told her. "Hey, thanks a bunch, you guys!" I added. "My locker looks amazing!"

Miss O hugged me back, a little harder than usual. "I got used to seeing you all the time over break, Juje. I'm going to miss you!" ("Juje" is what she calls me when she feeling especially sister-ish. It's pronounced "Ju-Gee.")

"Um, me too," I said. I couldn't help feeling a little weird with Noah standing right there, staring at us!

"Juje, huh?" he said with a smile. "Cute nickname!"

Omigod. Did Noah just say my nickname was cute?!

As my buds disappeared down the hall, and I found myself standing alone with Noah, I was suddenly struck with panic. I'd never actually hung around with a boy before—just the two of us I mean. Well, except for a few of my parents' friends' kids, but they were more like brothers to me than guys so it didn't count.

"So," I said.

"So," Noah repeated.

Way to be a dork, Juliette. Way to have an interesting conversation!

Ugh. And we'd been getting along so nicely up until now. I felt like I was about to blow it and spoil my chances of a new friendship with Noah by saying something incredibly lame. *Okay, Juliette! Think of something interesting to say! And quickly!*

"So, um, do you have any new classes this term?" I asked.

Oh, brother! No, no, no! Why had I said that? Talking about school was so lame!

Noah shrugged. "Yeah, I guess," he said. He looked down the hallway and I watched as he waved to some of his friends.

He wishes he were hanging with them, instead of standing here with me, I thought glumly.

"Well, I gotta get going," he said finally, shifting his backpack from one shoulder to the other. "I came in early to clean out my locker from last term and, well, I never made it down there."

"Oh! I'm sorry," I said.

We stood there in awkward silence.

What was wrong with me all of a sudden? I wondered. *I'd had plenty of conversations with boys before. Why couldn't I think of a single cool thing to say to Noah?*

"Okay, then," I said. "I'll see you around, I guess?"

Noah nodded. "Yeah. I guess," he said.

He started to walk away, then he spun back around. "Hey! Juje?" he called out with a grin.

I swallowed as I felt my face get hot. *He'd called me "Juje!" How cute was that?!?*

"Um, yeah?" I asked.

"Don't forget to turn off your cell," he called back. "You wouldn't want it to get taken away or anything."

"Right!" I called back. "Don't worry, I've already—" but he'd just spun around to greet his friends down the hall. "—turned it off," I mumbled. I watched him for a minute, then turned to face my new-and-improved locker. I felt like banging my head against the door.

Sheesh, Juliette! And the award for Most Uninteresting Girl goes to . . .

I stared at my reflection in my new periwinkle locker mirror. I can't believe what a dork I had turned into around Noah. I wished I had one of those "life remote-controls" like in that Adam Sandler movie. Then I could rewind the past ten minutes and start all over again with Noah. I know I could be much cooler the second time around.

Okay, Juliette! Time to get back into school mode! Time to forget about vacations and text message—and instead to think about history and algebra and . . .

I gazed at my new class schedule for second term, which Harlie had slipped into a clear plastic cover and stuck to my locker door with a periwinkle magnet.

. . . *Computer Clicks!* I finished. I really *was* excited about my new class. And the best part? I had it first period. The first class of the day.

I closed my locker door and pulled my black Abercrombie tote bag over my shoulder. (I was using the tote as my new school bag. It wasn't as comfortable as a backpack, but it was way cool.)

Heading for the computer lab, I tried to push all thoughts of Noah Sclar and his bouncing curls from my mind.

Focus, Juliette! I told myself. *Winter break is over! It's all about schoolwork now! Time to buckle down! Get good grades! No time for thinking about . . .*

And just as I was *about* to think the words "Noah Sclar," I bumped right into the guy!

"Hey Juje," Noah said. "Are you following me?"

My eyes widened and I became flustered all over again. "No! Um, I'm not—"

Noah let out a laugh. "Relax. I'm just joking. Where are you headed anyway?"

I took a deep breath and got hold of myself. "Computer Clicks," I managed to say.

"Me, too," he replied. "First period. Looks like we landed in the same class."

I nodded. "Looks that way," I said.

"Cool," Noah said. "That's a coincidence, don't you think?" He didn't wait for me to reply, instead he turned down the hallway and headed toward the computer lab. I followed behind him, watching his curls bounce as he walked.

"Uh, yeah," I muttered dreamily. "What a coincidence."

Chapter 2

Computer Clicking

Mr. Adams was everything I'd imagined he'd be . . . and more! Five minutes into class and I already knew I was headed for the best term at Sage *ever*. Not only was he so funny and smart, he was super-creative!

Right away he broke the twenty of us into groups of two in front of each computer station.

Wouldn't you know it—guess who I got paired up with?

Noah!

Really! I couldn't believe it at first, either. Am I lucky, or what? Now, hopefully, I'll get the chance to have a normal conversation with him. A conversation that won't include me blabbering on and on.

Noah fell into the seat next to me in front of "our" computer. "Hey Juje. Looks like we're sharing. Cool."

"Yup!" I managed. Unfortunately, my voice decided to come out an octave higher than usual, so my "Yup!" sounded more like a squeaky hiccup. Why is it as soon as I'm with Noah, all I can manage to say are things like, "Uh-huh" and "Yup?" anyway?

You should know that usually, I'm a pretty good conversationalist.

Thankfully, there was no real time for deep conversation. Mr. Adams got started right away, passing out an outline of what we'd be learning in his class during the term, then a permission slip for our parents to sign that would allow us to go on the school's Internet in class.

Looking over the outline, my heart soared when I read about our class projects. Each student had to complete a class project, something that is created on the computer. My eyes rested on one of Mr. Adams' suggestions—a project I *knew* I would be choosing: An online 'Zine!

A 'Zine is pretty much like a magazine, except that you read it online. It has pages like a regular magazine, and it's filled with articles and stories and stuff. I'd always wanted to create my own 'Zine, and now I would get the chance!

I could barely contain myself for the rest of class. I was so preoccupied with all the great 'Zine feature and article ideas racing through my head, I almost forgot I was sitting next to Noah and sharing a computer with him.

Well, *almost*. My heart *did* melt a little when he'd leaned over to me and whispered, "Dude, you're blocking the mouse pad."

That afternoon, Justine and Harlie walked home with Miss O, Isabella, and me. (Well, actually, Harlie *rolled* home with us on her Wheelys.) The girls were all coming over to hang at our house after school. Isabella happens to live down the block from me and Miss O, so it wasn't such a big deal for her, but since Harlie lives in New York City and Justine lives about twenty minutes away in the next town, they both had to get their parents' permission to come over.

As soon as we began the short walk home, I started telling the girls about my class project for Computer Clicks.

"What's a 'Zine exactly?" Isabella asked.

"It's a magazine. Online," Miss O told her before I could answer.

"So what was it like sitting next to Noah?" Harlie wanted to know.

So much for talking about the project!

"Um, I don't know!" I replied. I stared down at the ground as we walked, so the girls couldn't see my cheeks turn red at the mention of Noah's name.

"Come on, Juliette!" Harlie insisted. "You guys seemed pretty chummy at the lockers this morning."

I shrugged. "So?"

"So I think you have a crush on Noah Sclar!" Harlie replied.

I felt my cheeks get redder. "Do not!" I insisted.

"Then why are you blushing, Juliette?" Miss O asked with a grin.

"Come on, you can tell us!" Justine urged. "We're your BFFs!"

I sighed. True: A crush was definitely something you could trust to your BFFs. But the thing was, I wasn't really sure yet how I felt about Noah. "It's not a crush, *exactly*," I told them. "I mean, maybe it is! I don't know! But can we not talk about it?"

"So what if it's a crush?" Isabella asked. "Noah's cute! It would make sense to crush on him."

"Well, maybe I have a little, teensy, tiny crush on him," I admitted. "He's cute and all, but—"

"But *what*?" Harlie demanded.

"I just don't think we have that much in common," I said finally. "I mean he *is* way cute. But when it comes to just hanging out and talking, we have nothing to say to each other."

"Well," Miss O began diplomatically, "you only just started hanging together. Maybe when you get to know each other better, you'll find you have more things in common."

I nodded. "Maybe," I said. "I *do* think he has the most adorable curls!" I added dreamily.

Harlie let out a laugh. "Ha! Then there's something you and Noah have in common!" she announced. "You *both* think he has great curls!"

We all laughed as we bounded up the steps to our front door. I retrieved the house key from the mailbox and unlocked the door. Dad left the key in the mailbox on the days when Miss O and I would get home before my mother. She would be busy with daytime appointments but usually got home right after us. Usually, Mom arrived home a short time after we did.

It was too cold to have snacks out on the back deck today, so we dumped our bookbags and coats by the front door and headed into the kitchen. Harlie removed her wheels so that my mom wouldn't freak about scuffmarks on the floors.

"Your class project really sounds fun, Juliette," Miss O said, as she scanned the pantry for something good to eat.

"I know," I replied. "I want to get started right away, too. I want to make the coolest 'Zine ever!"

"Can we help?" Justine asked.

"Yeah, can we?" Isabella said.

"Really? You guys want to help me?" I asked them.

They all nodded. Even Harlie, who usually hates anything to do with writing, seemed eager to help with the 'Zine.

"Maybe I can make a comic strip for your 'Zine?" she suggested.

My eyes widened. "Omigod, Harlie! That would be excellent!" Harlie was a very talented comic book artist. She'd even created a comic superhero based on herself called Harlie Rox. A while back, we'd helped her paint a life-sized mural of Harlie Rox on the wall in her bedroom.

Harlie sat back proudly on her counter stool and grinned. "I think it would be fun to put Harlie Rox in your 'Zine."

"And I can take pictures around school," Justine offered. "Maybe ask kids questions like a roving reporter does? You know, like, 'What do you think of the food in the cafeteria?' And then we could put their pictures and their answers in the 'Zine in a column.

"Justine, that sounds like an excellent idea. I would love to have you take pictures for my 'Zine! I'm not so good with cameras."

Miss O let out a loud "*Hmpfh!*" and everyone laughed.

"What?" I demanded. "What's so funny?"

Miss O covered a plate with tortilla chips, and then covered the chips with shredded cheddar cheese and spices. "You're '*not so good*' with cameras?" she asked. "How about you *stink* with cameras?"

"Hey!" I protested. "No, I don't!"

Without a word, Miss O put the plate of nachos in the microwave and turned it on. Then she marched into our family room and pulled some envelopes out of the coffee table drawer. They were photos from our trip to Massachusetts last week. Photos that hadn't made it into the photo album. I watched as she tossed the envelopes on the counter.

Uh-oh.

The very first photo was one I had taken of Miss O and my parents at Gettysburg. Well, actually, truth be told, you couldn't exactly tell where they were because a big, blurry image of my finger covered half the picture.

"Hey! *That* was an accident!" I insisted, as the girls all made fun of my finger in the picture.

Everyone looked at me.

"Really! Someone bumped into me as I was pressing the button!"

"Oh, yeah?" Miss O asked casually. She flipped to the next picture in the pile. Again, my finger covered half the image.

Isabella giggled and leafed through the stack of photos. "Juliette! Your fingers got in the way of every single picture!"

I slumped in my seat. "Yeah, yeah," I muttered. "Okay, it's true. I'm the *worst* photographer *ever*."

Justine rushed to my defense and pointed to a beautiful shot of the Boston Harbor. "No, you're not so bad!" she said reassuringly. "Look. This one came out beautiful!"

"Ahem!" Miss O butt in. "*I* took that picture!"

Justine bit her bottom lip. "Ooops. Sorry, Juliette," she said. "Just trying to help."

"Okay, you guys!" I grumbled. "I get it! I stink at taking pictures, all right? Justine, the job is yours!"

"Thanks, Juliette!" Justine said.

I smiled at her. "No problem. Really. You're a zillion times better than me anyway. You're an excellent photographer—it only makes sense that you take the pictures for my 'Zine. I'll stick to what I do best: writing."

"That's true, Juliette," my sister chimed in. "You're the greatest writer we know!" I think she was trying to make nice with me after exposing my lame photography skills to everyone.

"Thanks," I replied.

"What about me?" Isabella asked. "What can I do for your 'Zine?"

I shrugged. "I don't know, Isabella. What would you like to do?"

Isabella thought for a second. "Oh! How about a sports page?" she asked. "I can report on the sporting events at school."

"Excellent idea!" I told her. "I think the kids at Sage will love reading about our teams and if they win or lose. That's the perfect job for you, too, since you know so much about basketball and volleyball and sports and stuff."

"And me?" Miss O asked. "What can I do?" She pulled the plate of nachos from the microwave and set them down on the counter for us to pick at. Then she looked at me pleadingly. "I want to do something for the 'Zine. Is there a job for me?"

Let me just stop right here and tell you something about my younger sister that you may not already know. Although she's only ten years old, she is, by far, the BEST cook (next to my Grandma Mimi) that I have ever met!

Take these nachos, for example. Most people would have just melted

cheddar cheese on tortilla chips and called it a day. But not my sister, the chef extraordinaire! She blends her own Mexican spices and mixes that in with the cheese just right. Then she tops it all off with homemade salsa!

From scratch!

I bit into a salty, cheesy chip and it was OMG unbelievable. "Miss O, these are delish!" I told her.

The others agreed. "Sososo yummy!" Isabella gushed.

"Thanks!" Miss O said proudly. "Actually, they're really simple to make, you know. You just need a little cumin and some cayenne. And you have to use fresh cilantro or they don't come out as good."

The girls and I exchanged dumbfounded looks.

"Um, excuse me, but are you speaking English?" I asked her.

Miss O blinked back at me in confusion. "What? Why?" she asked.

"Miss O!" Harlie cried with a laugh. "I've never even *heard* of cumin!"

"And cilantro?" Isabella asked. "What is that? A kind of cheese?"

My sister made a face. "Right. Sorry, guys! Sometimes I forget that not everybody knows all about cooking like I do. Cumin is a spice. And cilantro is like parsley, only more lemon-y."

"Wait! That's it!" Justine cried suddenly. "Miss O, you should do a recipe column for Juliette's 'Zine!"

My eyes widened. "Yes! With instructions on how to make super-yummy recipes! A new recipe each week! Great idea, Justine!"

Justine beamed. "Thanks!"

"Ooh, yes! I want to do that!" Miss O said eagerly. "Can I call it 'Miss O's Kitchen,' or, 'In the Kitchen with Miss O?' I know the perfect recipe for the first 'Zine. Homemade peanut butter cups!"

Harlie's eyes widened. "Hold on!" she announced, turning all serious-like. "You know how to *make* peanut butter cups?" she asked. "Dude, how long have I known you and not known this about you? I mean, I thought we were buds!"

Miss O rolled her eyes and sighed, "Okay, c'mon," she said, getting up from her stool and heading over to the pantry.

"What? Where?" Harlie asked in confusion.

"You're making me feel guilty!" Miss O said. "Now I *have* to make you peanut butter cups! C'mon! Right now!" She dragged Harlie across the kitchen, then pulled a roll of waxed paper out from a drawer. "Here! Start tearing off sheets. We need four of them. I'll go get the ingredients."

When my sister stepped away, Harlie turned to us and raised and lowered her eyebrows a few times in a sinister way. "Actually," she whispered to us with a sly smile, "she's made them for me before. I just wanted them again! *Heh-heh-heh!*"

The rest of us laughed.

"We'll never tell!" Isabella whispered back. "Not when homemade peanut butter cups are at stake!"

So while Miss O and Harlie made the peanut butter cups, and Isabella and Justine did their homework, I began to plan the first "issue" of my 'Zine. I decided I would include an article from me, a recipe column from Miss O, some pictures and interviews from Justine, a sports page from Isabella, and a comic strip from Harlie.

But I needed something else. Something that would make kids want to log on and read each week.

"Sunday," I announced to the girls as I glanced up from the notebook where I had been scribbling my ideas for the 'Zine.

"What about Sunday?" Isabella asked.

"I want to have a big 'Zine meeting here," I told them. "In the kitchen. We can bring our articles and pictures and stuff, scan them into the computer, then with Mr. Adams' help next Monday morning, I can launch the 'Zine on the Internet."

"Wow! So soon?" Miss O asked.

"It's a whole week. That's plenty of time," I assured her. "A whole week to get it all together."

"I guess," Miss O replied with a shrug. "Then okay, I'm down for Sunday."

"Me, too," the others chimed in.

This was going to be so great! I thought to myself with a smile. And my friends were so cool to jump in and help me out with the project. They were stoked about it, too! They really are the greatest.

And together, we were going to make the most awesome 'Zine that Mr. Adams, Noah, and everyone at Sage School had ever seen!

Chapter 3

Behind the 'Zines

On Sunday, at eleven o'clock in the morning, Justine's father dropped her off at our house. Isabella walked over a short time later, then we waited for Harlie. She had a gymnastics meet in the city and couldn't come over until noon. So instead of getting started on the 'Zine (Harlie would freak out if we started without her!) we hung out in Miss O's room and downloaded songs onto her iPod.

"This is so much fun!" Isabella said excitedly. But I noticed there was something sad about her voice.

"Is something wrong, Isabella?" I asked.

Isabella sighed. "It's my stepdad," she explained. "He never lets me do anything fun! I mean, *sheesh*! I'm going to be eleven soon, and he still won't let me use the Internet! I can't download any cool songs to my iPod, and I have to beg for permission to IM!"

Miss O put her arm around our friend's shoulder. "That stinks," she said sympathetically. "You can borrow my iPod if you want," she added.

Isabella smiled. "Thanks, Miss O. But it's not the same."

I felt so badly for Isabella. I didn't think I could live without my iPod or without IM'ing.

"Why don't you ask him to show you how to surf the 'Net?" I asked her. "Maybe if he sits with you a few times, he'll see that you are surfing responsibly."

"That's good advice, Juliette," Isabella replied. "I'll try that tonight."

The doorbell rang downstairs a little while later. At the same time we all jumped up and cheered, "Harlie!" Then the girls followed me downstairs.

But when I flung open the front door, instead of finding Harlie on the front porch, I found Tyler and Dana Brooks, the kids of my parents' best friends. Dad and Mr. Brooks worked together at a law firm in Westchester and Mom and Mrs. Brooks were on the PTA together at school.

"Oh!" I said in surprise. "Um, hey, Tyler. Hi, Dana. What are you guys doing here?"

Dana gestured to her family's SUV in the driveway. Her parents were just getting out of it. They waved to me.

"Hi, Juliette!" Mrs. Brooks called out. "How are you, honey?"

"I'm good!" I called back. "Come inside, guys," I told Tyler and Dana.

They followed me into the kitchen. "Mom!" I called downstairs to her office. "The Brookses are here!"

The Brookses lived close by and sent their kids to the Sage School, too. Dana is Miss O's age, and Tyler is a year older than me. But even though we were all so close in age, and would always do stuff together as families, Miss O and I would never really hang around with the Brooks kids in school. Only when our families would get together.

Truth be told, Miss O and I think Dana is a bit of a know-it-all. Not so much when we are hanging around with our families, but at school she can be pretty snobby. And Tyler? Well, let's just say he wasn't one of the most popular kids at Sage. I don't know why, exactly. I mean he's a nice guy and all, and he isn't bad looking. Maybe, I think, it's because he's a "techie." You know, one of those guys who are more interested in electronics and computers than in people? Like the kid the teachers always call on to assemble the projector, or to work the PowerPoint presentations?

"Do you guys know my friends?" I asked Dana and Tyler. "This is Justine and Isabella. Our other friend Harlie will be here any minute."

"Hey," they both said to the girls.

"So what's up?" I asked.

Dana shrugged. "Nothing, really," she said. "We were just coming back from the mall, and Dad wanted to stop off and see if your parents were home."

"Can I . . . um . . . put on the TV?" Tyler asked.

"The TV? Uh, sure. It's in the family room," I said.

"Yeah, I know," Tyler mumbled, hurrying out of the room.

Dana rolled her eyes as her brother left the room. "He is *obsessed* with that new music video channel," she said.

"Oh, me, too!" I said excitedly. "I watch it all the time—they have a new reality series on, kind of like *American Idol,* but different."

"I've seen that," Isabella said. "I love that channel, too. Wanna go watch until Harlie gets here?"

I nodded. "Sure. Let's go check it out."

My mom walked into the kitchen just then. "Hi, girls," she said. "Listen, the Brookses are going to join us for lunch. We're ordering in pizza and pasta. Is that okay with everyone?"

"Sure, Mom," I replied. "But no meat for Harlie," I reminded her. Harlie is a vegetarian.

"I know," Mom said.

The girls and I joined Tyler in the family room, just as my favorite show was starting.

"You like reality TV?" I asked Tyler.

"Um, yes," he replied. "*Survivor* is my favorite."

I smiled. "Hey! Mine, too!" I told him. "Miss O and I watch it every season. We don't miss a show! Who's your favorite survivor?" I asked.

"Um, Dan," Tyler said. "Because he is an astronaut."

"Juliette and I like Tom the Fireman," Miss O said. "Because he kicked butt, but also because he lives in Long Island, New York, near our grand-parents, Mimi and Poppy."

"Yeah, he was a decent player," Tyler said.

"Yuck!" Dana announced. "Don't you hate when they have to eat gross things?"

"Well, *Fear Factor* is much worse," I explained. "*That* is just the grossest show ever. Can you imagine being locked in a tank with bugs?" I shuddered, thinking about it.

"Or snakes?" Isabella asked. "Ewww!"

"I just think all reality shows are stupid," Dana went on.

Miss O's eyes widened. "Even *American Idol*?" she asked.

If you haven't guessed by now, my sister and I *are huge* reality TV fans. We watch, like, every reality show there is! *Survivor* and *American Idol* are our faves.

"Well," Dana admitted, "*American Idol* is okay."

"You know what I don't like about that show?" Justine asked us. "When it comes time to vote, I think a lot of people vote for the contestants who *look* the most like an idol, rather than the ones who sing the best."

"That's true," Isabella said.

"I think both are important!" Miss O said. "What do you think, Juliette?" she asked me.

They all turned to me and I had a huge smile across my face. "Forget what I think," I said. "But guess what? You guys have just given me the greatest idea for my first 'Zine article!"

"We did?" Miss O asked.

I nodded excitedly. "Yes! Especially since the Sage Sings competition is coming up soon. This article will be great! I can ask everyone to write in with their opinions: Is it more important to *look* like an American Idol, or *sound* like one?"

Isabella beamed. "Juliette, that's awesome! What a great idea!"

"Um, Juliette? You have a 'Zine?" Tyler piped up shyly.

"Not yet," I replied. "But I picked it for my class project for Computer Clicks. The girls are helping me put it together, but I'm the Editor-In-Chief."

"Are you using a Java script library?" Tyler asked.

I stared at him blankly. "Huh?"

"A Java script library," he repeated. "I have a great library source. For navigation bars, too," he added.

I looked at him in confusion. "What does that mean?" I asked.

Tyler's face reddened. "Um, you have to have Java and navigation components to run a 'Zine," he said.

"Oh. Well, I guess I'll learn that stuff in class," I replied. "I mean, Mr. Adams hasn't taught that to me yet," I explained.

"Do you want me to show you how to do it?" Tyler asked. "I have a bunch of reference programs and stuff at home. I could bring them over after school this week. Uh, if you want me to, that is."

"Oh! Um, sure," I said. "I guess. I mean, if you think I need all that."

Tyler nodded. "And how about a template and graphics?" he asked.

"I . . . don't . . . know," I stuttered, suddenly feeling anxious about the whole 'Zine thing. I didn't know about any of this technical stuff! How in the world was I going to launch my 'Zine tomorrow morning when I hadn't even learned about any of this stuff?

"Maybe Mr. Adams can show me how to do that tomorrow," I said.

"I can show you how to format the 'Zine," Tyler suggested. "I mean, if you want."

I shot a worried look at my friends.

"Do you think I should?" I asked Tyler. "Do you, um, really think you can help me?" I asked.

Tyler's cheeks turned red as he nodded. "Yeah! Sure! We can do it right now!"

"Right now?" I asked. "Uh, how long does it take?"

Before I knew it, Tyler had jumped up from the sofa and raced out to his

family's SUV. When he returned, he had his laptop and a huge bag filled with discs and cables and stuff.

"Uh, so, okay, I have three reference discs which will be good for looking up the HTML codes," he said as he plugged things into the wall and into my laptop, too. "And I have a whole box of pre-formatted CDs we can use to save stuff on."

"Yikes, Tyler," I said nervously. "It sounds kind of . . . complicated."

Tyler grinned. "Don't worry. I can show you how to do it all," he said. "I'm pretty good at computers."

Dana let out a snort as she walked into the kitchen. "You mean you are a computer *geek*," she commented.

I felt sort of bad for Tyler at the moment. I mean, he was trying to help me—and it seemed I really needed a ton of help!—and his sister was being sort of obnoxious.

"I think it's a good idea," I told Tyler. "Thank you so much! I don't know what I was thinking, launching a 'Zine tomorrow when I'm clearly not ready!"

"That's okay, Juliette," Tyler said. "I don't mind helping."

"So why don't we work together before lunch?" I asked. "Just us two. Then the others can help later."

Tyler beamed. "Okay, I'll set up the system in the kitchen. You have Wi-Fi?"

I stared at him blankly. "Uh, I'm not sure."

"I mean a wireless account," Tyler offered. "How do you normally connect?" he asked.

"To the Internet?" I asked.

He nodded.

"Oh, then yes, I think we have Wi-Fi. Uh, I'd better get my dad."

I left Tyler in the kitchen to set up his laptop, and then I went into the family room to find my father.

What was I thinking? I wondered.

How was I planning to launch my 'Zine tomorrow when I didn't have the slightest idea about any of this stuff?

I shook my head in amazement. Boy, I had my work cut out for me!

Harlie arrived at the same time as the pizza, and I filled her in on the plans for the day. I told her what Tyler had said about all the technical stuff I needed to know and Harlie looked as confused as the rest of us.

"So what do we do?" she asked before taking a bite of her vegetable pizza.

"So we take everything we have," I explained, "my blog, Miss O's recipe column, Isabella's sports pages, your comic strip, and Justine's student interviews, and we put them into a . . . " I couldn't remember what Tyler had called it.

"A *template*," Tyler said as he ate.

"Right. A template," I repeated. "It's like a puzzle frame, and all the articles are the pieces. Right, Tyler?"

Tyler nodded. "Yes," he said. "But you know what I think you should also have in your 'Zine, Juliette?" he asked.

Uh-oh—here comes some more technical stuff I've never heard of.

"What?" I asked.

"A science fiction blog!" he replied. His voice cracked as he went on to explain. "Where, like, *Star Trek* fans or *Star Wars* fans from all over the

country can log on, you know? And write to each other in Klingon? Or vote for their favorite *Star Wars* episode?"

Ugh. That was the worst idea I'd ever heard. I exchanged helpless looks with the girls around the table. Tyler had been super helpful so far, so I didn't want to hurt his feelings by telling him that his idea was dumb.

"Jeez, Tyler!" Dana declared. "You're such a geek sometimes! Nobody cares about that stuff!"

It was quiet for a moment, and I really didn't know what to say. I felt bad for Tyler, but I did, however, secretly agree with Dana.

"Um, thanks, Tyler!" I said finally. "But I think we're going to stick to topics that I'm more comfortable writing about. Being the Editor-In-Chief and all."

"Well, I could help you write it," Tyler offered. "And I know where to find all these cool Galactica graphics with spaceships that shoot lazers and stuff."

"Oh, brother!" Dana said, rolling her eyes.

I gulped. I was finally beginning to see why Tyler Brooks was *less than popular* at school.

"Uh, I don't think so, Tyler. But, thanks! Um, maybe in a future issue, okay? I just don't think it's the right topic for this 'Zine."

Tyler shrugged. "Okay," he mumbled.

"So," I said, anxious to change the subject, "I'd still like to put one more feature in my 'Zine. Something that kids will think is cool. Something interactive, maybe?"

"How about a fashion column?" Dana offered.

"I don't know," I hesitated. "I like the idea, but it doesn't sound very interactive."

Dana got up from the table. "Well, I tried," she shrugged. "I'm going to find Mom and Dad," she told Tyler. "To see if we're leaving soon." She left the room and we all exchanged looks.

"She's so moody sometimes," Tyler explained.

"That's okay," I told him. "I mean, I can't expect everyone to be psyched about *my* school project!"

"But she gets me so mad sometimes," Tyler went on. His face turned a little red. "She acts like such a know-it-all and it's so embarrassing."

Miss O and I exchanged looks—mostly because we secretly thought the same thing about Dana!

"Maybe you can talk to her," I suggested. "You know, when things are going good? That's a better time to bring up problems you have with someone," I told him. "Rather than when things are bad—because then the other person can become defensive."

Tyler glanced at me. "Yeah," he said. "That's true. I should try that."

"Like maybe when you're hanging out, watching a funny movie and getting along," I went on, "just tell her, 'You know, I wanted to talk to you about something.'"

"You should definitely try that," Isabella urged. "Juliette knows what she's talking about! She's an excellent advice-giver!"

"The best," Miss O added. "I should know—I live with her!"

I smiled. "Thanks, guys."

Harlie took a sip of her lemonade. "You know what I'm thinking, Juliette?" she said with a mysterious expression.

"No, what?"

"I'm thinking we just found the perfect feature for your 'Zine," she said.

"Huh?" I asked. "What do you mean?"

"An advice column!" Harlie cried. "You know, like, 'Dear Juliette,' or something like that. Kids can write in with their problems, and you can fix 'em!"

"Oooh, good idea, Harlie!" Isabella said. "She's right, Juliette. Just like you helped me with advice about my stepdad and the Internet. You can help whoever writes in with a problem."

Know what? My friends were on to something. An advice column was an excellent idea. And I could start the first column with the advice I'd just given to Tyler. Or, Isabella could write in a problem with her stepdad and I could write back. I would change their names, of course, and keep the whole thing anonymous.

I scribbled some notes in my notebook, then slammed the book shut.

"Thanks to Harlie's great idea," I announced, "we are officially ready to create the first 'Zine! Thanks so much, you guys! We can start typing all the articles into the template Tyler loaded in for me, and then we can download Justine's pictures and scan in Harlie's comic strip. Tomorrow morning I'll ask Mr. Adams to show me how to launch it onto the Internet."

"Glad we could help!" Harlie replied, leaning back in her chair confidently.

"Tyler," I said, "I really owe a lot to you! I don't know what I would have done if you hadn't helped me today!"

Tyler's face turned red. "Well, thanks," he said.

A second later, Dana and her parents came into the kitchen.

"We're going to be on our way," Mrs. Brooks announced. "It was so nice to see you, girls," she added.

"Nice to see you, too, Mrs. Brooks," I replied. "And thanks for bringing Tyler over!" I added. "He saved my school project! And he saved me from what might have been a big embarrassment tomorrow in class!"

Tyler smiled and looked down as he packed away his computer and programs. "It wasn't such a big deal," he said. "I just helped you format and code stuff."

When they'd left, I helped clear off the dining room table from the pizza party. I flipped open my laptop and loaded one of the CDs Tyler had made for me.

"Ready to get cracking?" I asked the girls.

"You bet!" Miss O said.

"Ready!" Isabella chimed in. "Do you want me to write a letter asking you for advice?" she asked. "You know, for the column?"

I nodded eagerly. "Yes! I need that right away!" I told her. "I have a lot to plug into the template Tyler gave me."

"Can *we* give *you* just a bit of advice before we begin?" Miss O asked.

"Hey—that's *my* job, I thought!" I joked.

"Right. Ha! No, really," Miss O said.

I eyed my sister suspiciously. "What is it?" I asked.

Miss O and the others exchanged looks. "Okay. Here it goes," she said. "Take it one step at a time!" she cautioned me.

I blinked. "What do you mean?"

"Well," she said. "You know how . . . *intense* . . . you can be when you're working on a project," she said.

"Yeah? So?" I demanded.

"What I'm trying to say," she said, "is don't go all 'Juliette' on us."

"Huh? What does that mean?" I wanted to know.

Miss O folded her arms across her chest. "Listen, I'm just following the advice you gave to Tyler before! I'm bringing this up while you're in a good mood, so don't get defensive!"

My sister was right. I should be following my own advice—if I was going to be an advice columnist from now on.

"Okay," I said, taking a deep breath. "Shoot. What does 'going all Juliette' mean?"

"Well," Isabella said gently, "it's just that your *intensity* sometimes makes us all nuts. Like that time you got so crazy entering the radio slogan contest for The Ices Shoppe?"

I remembered. "Did I make you nuts then?" I asked with a gulp.

The girls exchanged looks.

"Well, it *was* kind of crazy to IM me in the middle of the night with your ideas," Harlie remarked.

My face turned red. "Yeah, I guess you're right. Sorry about that."

"No problem," Harlie said.

"And maybe you shouldn't wake me up at five o'clock in the morning to read me a list of your ideas," Miss O added. "*That* was going all 'Juliette' on me!"

"But you told me to tell you when I got something good!" I protested.

"Yeah, but you could have waited until, I don't know, *dawn* to tell me!"

"Yeah, I guess," I said in embarrassment. "That was totally obnoxious to wake you up."

"And don't boss us around," my sister added.

"Hey!" I protested. "I'm not bossy!"

"Right. You're the best! A terrific sister!" Miss O said. "Just *please*, try to keep it fun around here, okay?"

My friends looked at me with pleading expressions while I mulled over what they'd just said.

Was I that much of a monster?

"Okay," I said finally. "You got it. All fun. No stress. I promise!"

Miss O grinned. "Thanks, Juliette!" she said. "You know I love you," she added.

"Yeah, whatever," I mumbled. "And you're like a sister to me," I told her.

Miss O smiled.

"Thanks! Wait—*Hey!*" she said, as the rest of fell into a heap of laughter.

Hours later, after we'd retyped everything into the template Tyler had downloaded for me, and after everyone's parents had come to get them, I was almost finished.

Next came the part where I could pick cool clip art to juice up the pages.

I checked the clock in the kitchen, and it was almost ten o'clock at night. I also needed to find a nice font for my advice column, since the one I had chosen earlier was too big and made the text run onto another page. I tried to make it smaller, but when I did, you couldn't read it.

I tried one last time to change the size of the font and got the message: ERROR WARNING for the one hundredth time!

"Dad!" I wailed.

Luckily, my father knew a little bit about computers. More than me

anyway! He came into the kitchen and showed me what I was doing wrong.

"You need to highlight all the text," he said. "Then you click on the font you want, and click 'update.'"

"Okay. Got it!" I said, highlighting the advice column. But it was late, and I was tired, and so, when I went to click "update," I accidentally clicked "delete."

The advice column that I'd worked so hard on disappeared.

"Oh, no!" I cried. "Can I get that back?"

Dad frowned. "I don't think so, sweetheart. You'll have to re-type it."

I rubbed my eyes with the palms of my hands. This can't be happening, I thought.

"*Aaarrrrggghhh!*" I cried, just as Miss O walked into the kitchen.

"Aren't you finished yet?" she asked with a yawn.

"No! And I just lost the whole advice column!" I wailed in frustration.

Miss O's eyes widened. "No way! That stinks!"

"What are you still doing up?" I asked my sister.

"I was talking to Harlie online," she replied. "She couldn't believe you were still up, working on the 'Zine."

I glanced at the clock again. "I know," I said sleepily. "I've been doing this all day!"

"Why don't you take a break, Juliette?" Miss O asked. "You don't *have* to launch the 'Zine tomorrow, you know. You have the whole term to do this project!"

"I know, but I really want Mr. Adams to see what a great job I can do and what a good writer I am!" I explained. "I want to be the first one to finish the class project!"

"That's admirable, Juliette," Dad said as he poured himself a glass of water. "But this project shouldn't be at the expense of the rest of your schoolwork."

"I know."

"Let's go, Miss O," he said. "Up to bed, please."

"Okay, Dad." She gave me a comforting pat on the back, then headed for the stairs. "See you in the morning, Juje," she said.

"Wait a sec!" I called to her.

"What?" she asked from the bottom of the steps.

"Are you thinking up ideas for your next column?" I asked. "I'm going to need it pretty soon, you know."

Miss O didn't answer me at first. "Well, I hadn't actually thought about it," she replied. "I was, um, going to sleep."

"Please, Miss O!" I cried. "I need all the help I can get with this! And now I have to re-type this whole column into the template again, and then I still have to change the fonts and the colors . . . "

"Okay! I'll start thinking of my next column, Juliette," Miss O assured me. "I promise . . . I won't be late. Good night!"

"And tell Harlie I'll need her next comic strip in a few days!" I called to her as she went up to bed. "Tell her now, Miss O! Send her an IM!"

I turned back to my computer screen and sighed. I checked the clock a third time, then looked at the list of things I still needed to do to have the 'Zine ready for Mr. Adams tomorrow morning.

It was going to be a long, long night.

Chapter 4

Hit or Miss?

"I don't know what's wrong, Mr. Adams!" I cried out in a panic. "My Dad and I were up last night until midnight putting the 'Zine together! The file has to be here somewhere!"

I punched the keyboard like crazy, but all that kept coming up on my computer screen was: FILE NOT FOUND.

Mr. Adams shook his head. His expression was sour and it totally freaked me out because he was usually so cheerful.

"Juliette, I'm very disappointed in you," he said.

My heart sank.

"Your teachers last term had such nice things to say about your work, but unfortunately I'm not impressed. You are nothing but irresponsible in my class."

I felt tears come to my eyes as I frantically searched the document files for my 'Zine. Could I have accidentally erased the whole file? I wondered. Deleted it by mistake, when I'd meant to save it?

Could all my hard work . . . be gone forever?

"Wait! Please wait!" I pleaded. "It's got to be here somewhere!"

In the chair next to me, Noah shook his head in disgust. He was probably so embarrassed to be lab partners with me—the Queen of Lameness! This was the worst day of my life. I continued to click and type, click and type, click and type. But all that came up was:

FILE NOT FOUND
FILE NOT FOUND
FILE NOT FOUND
FILE NOT FOUND

"Give it a rest, Juliette!" Noah whispered harshly.

"But . . . but . . . I want Mr. Adams to see what a great job I did!" I told him. "I can't fail at this project! I . . . I . . . I can't give up!"

"Give up!" Noah insisted.

"Give up!" Mr. Adams agreed.

"Just give up, Juliette! Give up! Give up . . ."

I felt someone shake my shoulder.

"Wake up, Juliette! Wake up! Wake up!"

Huh?

"Come on, Juliette! We've got to get going!"

I bolted upright and blinked in confusion.

"Dreaming?" I croaked in a morning voice.

"No duh!" Miss O retorted. "I tried to wake you up twice already! Isabella will be here in ten minutes to walk to school!"

I leapt out of bed. "Yikes! Ten minutes!" I exclaimed. "Oh, man! Why didn't you wake me?" I tried to rub the sleep out of my eyes.

My sister groaned. "I *did* try!" she insisted. "But you were out cold. What time did you finish last night anyway?"

I quickly pulled on a pair of jeans and a clean T-shirt. Then I layered a cropped sweatshirt over the T-shirt, so the tee stuck out from below. "Uh, I think eleven-thirty," I said with a yawn. "But the 'Zine looks great so far. You should see it!"

"No time this morning. We have to meet the girls by the "doorz" like we promised!"

"Right," I said as I peered into the mirror. The "doorz" are the double doors by the Sage School entrance near the gym. Since my second year at Sage, Miss O and I have been meeting Isabella, Justine, and Harlie there before school every morning. Mostly we just hang out and talk before first period, but it's become our "thing."

Last night, before their parents came to pick them up, I'd asked the girls if they'd help me out and make posters advertising the website address for my 'Zine to hang up all around school, so kids would know where to find it when they went online that night. Each of them agreed to make two posters for me.

Do I have the *bestest* friends, or what?

But, *yikes!* What was I going to do about my hair? It was a total mess this morning. I sprayed some detangler on it, brushed a little, and then

searched my dresser for my favorite headband. "Where's my denim Undees band?" I asked my sister.

"Dunno," Miss O replied. "I didn't borrow it," she added.

Then I remembered it was hanging in my locker on one of my new hooks. I would have to grab it before first period, if I didn't want the whole school to see me with severe bed head.

I brushed my teeth and grabbed my jacket. It was a world record—I had managed to get ready in ten minutes flat! But I couldn't be late to meet the girls at the "doorz" this morning. Especially since I had asked them to meet me there.

I was ready for the walk to school just as Isabella appeared on our driveway. She lives three houses down, and her mother lets her walk by herself to meet Miss O and me every morning, then we walk to school together.

Isabella struggled a little, trying to manage her book bag and the posters she'd made, so I offered to carry her posters.

"Sure!" she said. "That would be great."

When we were all set, we started off down the street. My mom used to watch us walk to the end of our block, but she doesn't do that anymore. I guess now that we're older, she trusts us to walk on our own.

When we got to the "doorz," Justine and Harlie were already there.

"My father drove me to school today!" Harlie announced. "Mainly because I couldn't manage with these posters and my book bag on the bus."

"Really?" I asked her. "That was nice of him!"

"Well, actually, he had to take my mother to her doctor's appointment

anyway, so it all worked out," Harlie reported. Harlie's mother is pregnant and goes to her doctor once a month to check on the baby. Harlie is going to have a baby sister in July! We're all so stoked about that.

"So, what do you think?" Justine asked as she unrolled a very long banner and held it up for us to see. It was so long that Miss O and I had to grab one end to help hold it open.

The banner was amazing! I couldn't believe how much work Justine had put into it! She'd cut out big block letters—each a different color—from construction paper, then glued them on a poster-sized roll of paper to spell out my 'Zine's Web address. Then she'd used glitter glue around the border. She had really worked hard on it!

"Justine, I love it!" I cried. "It's *awesome!*"

"Wow, Jus!" Miss O added. "I couldn't have done it better." That was truly a compliment coming from my sister, the talented artist who has an art studio in her bedroom.

Harlie was about to show us her posters, which she'd made on Day-Glo colored poster board, when, to our surprise, Dana Brooks appeared at the "doorz."

"Hey, Miss O!" she said cheerfully. "Hey, guys!"

"Hi, Dana!" Miss O said. "I'm glad you came! We were just showing Juliette the posters we made for her project. Look at what Justine made," she added.

Dana's eyes widened as Justine and Miss O rolled open the banner again. "That's unbelievable," she said. "You made that all by yourself?"

Justine nodded proudly.

"Wow. I stink at arts and crafts," she muttered. "I wish I could make something like that."

Harlie held up one of her posters. "And I made this," she announced proudly. It was a big drawing of Harlie Rox (the superhero) and it said:

Harlie Rox Appearing In This Week's Sage Zine Zcene! The Coolest Internet 'Zine On This Planet . . . Or Any Other!

"Ha! That's funny, Harlie!" I said with a laugh. "I love it!"

Harlie grinned, then took a bow. "Thank, you, thank you!" she said. "To all my adoring fans, thank you!"

Miss O rolled her eyes playfully. "You're such a pillow-head," she joked, calling Harlie the silly name we used to call each other as kids.

"Am not!" Harlie retorted.

"Are so!" Miss O replied with a laugh. "Anyway, changing the subject, I asked Dana to meet us here," my sister explained. "She said she'd help out with the posters."

"Thanks, Dana," I said. "That would be really great."

"No problem," Dana shrugged. "But I don't know how much help I'll be," she added. "I'm not a great artist or writer or anything."

"Can you use scotch tape?" Miss O asked her.

Dana scoffed. "Well, duh! Of course I can use tape," she replied.

"Then you're hired!" Miss O said cheerfully. "All we need is some help with hanging the posters all over school."

"I can do that," Dana said.

"And, we need help passing out these fliers to other kids," Miss O went on. "I made the original last night and Mom printed out one hundred copies for us to hand out."

"This looks pretty cool, Juliette," Dana said. "I'm going to visit your 'Zine today."

"Um, well, it's not exactly up yet," I told her.

The girls all looked at me.

"But I thought you were launching it this morning?" Justine asked.

"We made all these posters," Harlie added.

"No, I know!" I told them. "It's okay. I mean, it's still going to launch this morning. I first need Mr. Adams to help me."

"Should we wait then, before handing out the fliers?" Isabella asked.

"No!" I replied. "Let's just get them out. I want everybody to know about it."

Miss O shrugged. "Okay, Juliette. If you think we should."

I nodded, but I had the strangest feeling in my gut. Something that told me I really should wait until the 'Zine was up and running before I hung up the posters and passed out the fliers.

But I couldn't wait. I was so excited! I was positive it would be ready to launch this morning anyway.

We divided up the fliers and the tape, then split up into groups of two (Isabella was with me, Miss O was with Dana, and Harlie and Justine). We each took a section of the school building.

Since middle division is in a separate building across the street, Isabella came with me there to hang up the posters and pass out fliers.

I found an excellent place for one of Isabella's posters right at the entrance to the building. Every student had to pass through this way, so it was a prime location.

"Your 'Zine is going to be the coolest!" Isabella said as I was taping a poster to the wall. "And you're going to be so popular!"

"Ha!" I said with a laugh. But it was a nice thought anyway.

"I just hope Mr. Adams can help me put it up on the Internet today," I told her. "So that kids can visit it as soon as they get home from school."

Just then, the warning bell rang loudly.

"Oh! I have to get back across the street," Isabella said. "I don't want to be late!"

"Okay. Thanks for helping me, Izzy! You're the best!" I said.

"No problem," she replied. "That's what BFFs are for, right?"

"Right!"

"I'll see you later, Juliette," she called out as she raced down the path toward the lower division building.

After Isabella left, I headed for my locker to dump off the roll of tape and the extra fliers. (Yes, and to find my emergency denim hair band!)

Along the way, I handed a few fliers out to some kids in the hall. It was funny to see them all checking out the fliers and posters. Kind of exciting, too!

But as I made my way to Computer Clicks class that morning, I still had that weird feeling sitting there in the pit of my stomach. I'll bet it had to do with that awful nightmare I'd had, where Mr. Adams and I were trying to launch my 'Zine and everything just kept going wrong.

Why was I worrying so much? I wondered. My 'Zine had come out pretty good, I thought. Dad had said so, too. True, I didn't know yet if it would be successful, and if kids would like it or not, but I knew, deep down, I had given it my very best effort. As for how successful it might be . . . I wouldn't know that until after it launched and after I checked to see how many "hits," or visits, the 'Zine had received.

I guess I was feeling so yucky because the thought of disappointing my favorite teacher was so horrible. Especially since I wanted him to think I had enough talent to become an ace reporter just like him!

I only hoped that my dream this morning wasn't any indication of what was really going to happen.

When I arrived to class, Mr. Adams agreed to sit with me and go over the basic HTML language we'd learned last week. You have to know that stuff pretty well in order to develop something to put on the Internet. It's funny how they call it a "language," but that's really what it is. You have to "translate" everything you do into HTML language so the computer understands it.

To me? HTML might as well have been Swahili. I didn't really get it, but Mr. Adams said he would show me just enough that I needed to know in order to put my 'Zine on the 'Net.

"Let's see what you have so far," Mr. Adams said, pulling up a chair at the computer station Noah and I shared.

"Okay," I said. I pulled open my tote bag and dug inside for the disc I had saved my 'Zine on.

"I worked all weekend on this," I added, hoping I'd sounded more confident than I'd felt.

I handed Mr. Adams the disc and he slipped it into the computer drive.

"The file is called 'Juje,'" I explained. Noah looked on as Mr. Adams scanned the files. He found it, then clicked to open the file.

Something looked odd about that file, I thought, as we waited for it to load and open. And before I could stop it, I realized what was wrong: Mr. Adams had opened a photo file called "Juje" and not a document file called "Juje."

My bad, because there were two files named Juje, and I'd forgotten. And worse, the file that was opening at that very second was the file of vacation photos I had taken on our trip to Gettysburg. You know, all those pictures of my thumb?

"Wait!" I cried as the photos appeared one by one on the computer screen.

But it was too late. Mr. Adams and Noah were already both studying my awful pictures!

"What the—?" Noah began.

Mr. Adams made a face and leaned back in his chair. "Is this," he asked, pointing to a photo of my father and mother—and, yes, my thumb—in front of a memorial statue, "is this what you want to download?"

I gulped as I felt my face redden. "Um, no, Mr. Adams," I said quietly. "That's the wrong file. Those are pictures from vacation."

Noah let out a chuckle. "Looks like pictures of your thumb," he said dryly. "Where'd you go on vacation? The Finger Lakes?"

He and Mr. Adams had a good laugh over that.

"Ha, ha," I said, taking control of the mouse. (This was *so* embarrassing.) "Um, this is the right file, I think," I said, clicking on the file that said, "Juje.doc."

Thankfully, a second later, the files for my 'Zine came onto screen. I breathed a sigh of relief. I hadn't lost them all.

"Okay then," Mr. Adams said. "It looks like you have all the files and you are ready to launch," he said. "I'm pretty impressed, Juliette," he added.

"How did you know how to format all this? And where did you learn how to use this program?"

I grinned. "My friend is a computer expert," I told him. "We worked together all day yesterday!"

Mr. Adams clicked around a little while longer, explaining to me everything he was doing as he did it. "Let's translate this to HTML and let's configure this, this and this . . . "

I watched and took notes the whole time. By the end of the period, Mr. Adam's announced, "Juliette, you are now ready to launch!"

Wow! I couldn't believe it! This was so exciting!

"Great!" I said excitedly.

He handed me a worksheet with instructions, and I officially "launched" my 'Zine just as the bell for class rang.

I sat back in my seat and breathed a sigh of relief.

Let the hits begin!

That afternoon at three-fifteen, I flew through the front door and raced upstairs to my bedroom. Had anybody visited my 'Zine yet? I wondered. I know it had only been on the Web since this morning, and that kids were just about getting home from school, but I was just so anxious, I couldn't wait. I crossed my fingers as I bolted up the steps. I know that's a silly superstition, but whatever.

Wouldn't you know it, when I pushed open the door to my bedroom, I found my mother on my computer!

"Mom!" I cried. "I need to get online!"

"Well, that's a nice way to say hello to your mother," she said as she typed on my keyboard.

I growled quietly in frustration, and then cleared my throat. "Um, sorry, Mother dear!" I said, my voice dripping with sweetness. "Sorry, kind lady who buys me stuff, cooks for me, and washes my clothes! How are you this wonderful afternoon?" I asked. "That better?"

Mom laughed. "Much," she replied. "I'm fine. But it's actually your father who does the laundry," she added.

"Whatever!" I groaned. "Mom, I *need* to get online!"

"Okay, okay! I'm just logging off, Juliette," Mom said. "My computer downstairs was acting up today, so I had to use yours for work."

"I hope you didn't change my settings!" I said worriedly.

"Don't worry, I didn't change a thing," she replied as she gathered up all her reports and papers.

"Good!"

"Oh, but I *did* IM everyone on your Buddy List and tell them how much you love pretty princesses and unicorns."

"Ha-ha," I said dryly. "Not funny!" Well, it *was* sort of funny because my mother also knew how much I hated princess-y, pink, girly, unicorn-type things! Even when I was three, I preferred to play with cars and trucks, rather than dolls. I never once owned a doll, though I *did* secretly wish I had "News Anchor Barbie" when I was seven.

As soon as Mom was finished, I called Miss O into my room and I entered the address for the 'Zine, and my secret password, and then we waited breathlessly.

"Hurry, already!" I said excitedly.

Finally, the 'Zine appeared. I watched as the Home Page came into view and a smile broke out across my face.

"Oh, wow, Juliette!" Miss O gushed. "That is so cool! And you made the background *periwinkle*!" she added. "Nice touch!"

"Thanks," I said with a smile. It did look pretty great.

"Oooh, this is so exciting!" my sister cooed. "I've never been published online before!"

I shot her a look.

"Okay, I've never been published *anywhere* before," she corrected herself. "But it's still exciting!"

Before I could check the "hits" counter (that's like a little speedometer on the Web site that counts each time someone visits), my Buddy List appeared with a flash. The next thing I knew, I was getting an IM.

JUSTme713: OMG, Ju! Looks gr8!

It was from Justine. Obviously she had just seen the 'Zine.

jujuBEE: thanx, jus. Glad u likey!
JUSTme713: AWESOME! :)

Suddenly, another IM box appeared.

harliegirl95: Woo-hoo! Awesome ZINE, grlfrnd!
jujuBEE: u know it, dude! TTYL

I signed off from my Buddy List so Miss O and I could check out the 'Zine without any more interruptions. This was so exciting! I couldn't wait to see how many people had visited my 'Zine!

I scrolled down the Home Page toward the "hits" counter Tyler had downloaded for me.

Miss O breathed over my shoulder as we watched the screen. "Can't you go faster?" she asked.

Before I could reply, the hits counter appeared:

0000002

"Two?" Miss O and I both cried out.

"Two hits?" I said in disbelief.

"Well," Miss O said, trying to sound cheerful about it. "It's still early, you know. And two is good, Juliette! That means two people saw the posters and logged on to read your 'Zine!"

I didn't answer her because I noticed there was a number "2" next to "Comments" on my 'Zine menu.

"Look, those two people commented on the 'Zine," I said. "Let's check out what they say."

I clicked "Comments" and a new periwinkle screen appeared. I frowned when I read it.

COMMENTS: LOVED YOUR 'ZINE! VERY INTERSTING AND COOL! JUSTINE

COMMENTS: AWESOME 'ZINE! THIS 'ZINE ROX!!! LATER, HARLIE

Oh, great. Both hits were from my BFFs! So actually, nobody new had visited my 'Zine at all.

That yucky feeling was back.

Miss O put her hand on my shoulder. "Sorry, Juliette," she said. "But let's check again later, after dinner. Maybe a lot of kids aren't home from school yet. Or maybe they had afterschool activities or something."

"Yeah. Maybe," I replied.

But that yucky feeling grew.

What if no one visits?

What if my 'Zine project ends up being a huge disaster?

Just like in my dream last night???

Chapter 5

Dreading Class

Miss O came bouncing into my bedroom at seven a.m. the next morning. "So?" she asked breathlessly.

"Three," I replied glumly.

"You mean we got one more hit?" she asked excitedly. "Well, that's *something*! Come on! I mean, yeah, it's slow, but you got one more and—"

"It's from *Isabella*," I said, cutting her off. "Her stepdad must have let her go online last night."

Miss O was quiet. "Oh," she said finally. "Well—"

"Never mind," I told her. "I'm just going to have to face the truth. That my 'Zine project may not have been such a great idea!"

Miss O gave me a hug. "Well, I think it's great," she said. "And not just

because I have a recipe column in it," she added. "I think it's an awesome idea and it came out so great!"

"Thanks, Miss O. I know you're trying to cheer me up," I told her. She really was an excellent sister.

"Maybe we need more posters?" she said thoughtfully. "I'll go e-mail the girls to tell them we need an emergency arts and crafts lunch meeting today at school. We can have lunch in the all-purpose room and make more fliers and posters while we eat."

I smiled at my sister and nodded. "You guys are the best," I said. "Come on. Let's get ready for school. I don't want to talk about 'Zines or hits or even computers any more this morning," I added, snapping off my computer screen.

"No problem!" Miss O said. "How about pancakes? Can we talk about pancakes?"

I raised one eyebrow. "Only if they're chocolate chip pancakes," I replied.

Miss O grinned. "Chocolate chip pancakes coming right up!" she announced. "But the best I can do is microwave the frozen kind. No time for scratch."

"Still good," I told her.

I followed her out of my room and down to the kitchen. My sister was being super sweet this morning, but I had a feeling even chocolate chip pancakes weren't going to cheer me up.

Ever since the first day of second term, when I found out that Noah and I were in the same first period, I've looked forward to going to class every day. True, after one week of classes together our conversations hadn't grown much beyond, "Hey, what's up?" "Nothing, what's up with you?" but I still really liked getting to sit and share a workstation beside him for fifty minutes each day. He was so cute and he could be kind of funny sometimes.

Okay. So maybe my crush *was* getting bigger!

Anyway, this particular morning, I was wishing Noah and I weren't partners. Especially since I was about to be humiliated right in front of him. Mr. Adams planned on presenting my 'Zine in front of the class this morning. With Noah sitting at the same computer, he was going to see every single embarrassing moment. Like the part about how my 'Zine had only received three hits in the first day.

In the wide world of the Web, that translated into a big ol' *flop*.

When I walked into the classroom that morning, I found Noah bent over the keyboard typing furiously.

"Hi," I said, sitting in the seat next to him.

"Hey, Juliette," he said. "Wassup?"

"Nothing," I replied. "What are you working on?" I asked.

Noah looked up from the keyboard. "Check this out," he said. "It's my project. Mr. Adams is checking to see how all our projects are coming along this morning. Did you know that?"

No duh, I thought to myself glumly.

"Yes," I told him. "How's yours coming along?" I asked. Noah chose to develop a Webpage for his project. He'd been talking about it all week. It had something to do with listing all of the songs his band, As If, knew how to play.

Noah grinned. "Coming along excellent," he said. "Wanna see?"

I nodded and Noah opened the Webpage. Though he hadn't added any graphics to the page yet, the font he had chosen was nice.

"Looks cool," I told him.

Noah sat back proudly. "Thanks," he replied.

"My first issue is finished," I said. "I mean, it's up and running, but . . . nobody seems to be visiting."

"Bummer," Noah said.

"Well, I think once people know about it, they'll visit," I said. "My friends and I are going to make some more posters today."

Just then, Mr. Adams appeared at our station. "Good morning, Juliette. Noah," he said. "Are you ready to show us all what you've been working on?"

Noah nodded eagerly. I managed a small nod, too. Mr. Adams had obviously seen some of my project yesterday when he'd helped me launch it on the Web. But in just a few minutes he—not to mention the whole entire class—would see my pathetic hits counter, so I was preparing for big-time embarrassment.

"Okay, great!" Mr. Adams said. "Noah, let's see what you've got so far. And Juliette, I'm especially eager to see how your 'Zine did on its first day," he added.

I gulped. *Not too eager*, I hoped.

Noah clicked the mouse and his Webpage appeared. He turned up the volume on the computer and as the page loaded, we could hear As If playing a Dave Matthews song. Everyone from the other workstations came over to check out Noah's project along with Mr. Adams.

"So let's say you wanted to know all the songs we play," Noah

explained, "you can click here and the list will come up. Then, if you click this, you can read all about me and the other guys," he said. "I'm going to put in all the four-one-one about each band member. The total package on As If," he said proudly.

I laughed quietly to myself. It was just funny to hear Noah talk so seriously.

"Very nice, Noah!" Mr. Adams commended him. "Great work. I think you had better sign up for a few computer lab sessions after school," he added, "to work with me on getting the technical stuff set up."

Noah nodded. "Okay, Mr. Adams," he said. "I will."

"Okay. Now, Juliette! Let's see what you've got."

My heart sank as I realized the entire class was going to hang around to see my project, too. Ugh! Every kid was going to see my pathetic hits counter: 00003! I started to wish I had spent last night calling everyone I knew to beg them to visit the Web site, just so the hits counter would go higher.

I felt slightly panicky as I typed my Web address into the navigation bar. I silently prayed that this wouldn't end up being *too* humiliating.

"Okay," I said, clearing my throat. "Here it goes. This is my 'Zine. It's called the Sage Zine Zcene."

My periwinkle home page appeared, and a few kids immediately reacted.

"Ooooh, sweet!" someone commented.

"Looks nice," Mr. Adams said.

"Cool," someone else muttered.

"'Zine Zcene,'" another person read out loud, "cool name."

"Thanks," I said. Then I clicked around, giving them all a little tour of the 'Zine and its features: My blog, Miss O's recipes, the advice column,

Justine's photos, and Harlie's comic strip. My hand shook a little, though, as I scrolled down the home page, toward the hits counter . . .

"I only just launched the 'Zine online yesterday," I explained, "so, it, um, hasn't really had a chance to catch on, but I think that maybe in a few weeks—"

A boy in my class, Samson Brennan, suddenly cut me off.

"Wow!" he cried. "Twenty-one hits! That's awesome!"

Huh? Twenty-one what?

My eyes fell on the hits counter, which now indeed read twenty-one. I stared at the number in complete shock.

00021

There it was. No joke! I couldn't believe eighteen new people had visited my 'Zine since I'd checked it an hour ago!

I quickly glanced up to check the "Comments" section. To my surprise, it said that ten people had posted comments about my 'Zine!

OMG! Ten comments!!!

"Nice, Juliette," Mr. Adams said. "I think your 'Zine is coming along nicely. As the 'Zine Host *and* Editor-In-Chief, you have a lot of work ahead of you. Especially with so many interactive elements," he added. "Great work . . . so far."

I was speechless. "Um, thanks!" I managed to say.

"The tough part," he went on, "will be trying to maintain your 'Zine. The Host has the difficult job of reading and responding to all the posted comments. When you open your 'Zine up to the community like that, you'll be surprised by how many people respond. Hopefully, you're up for the challenge of maintaining your 'Zine."

I nodded. "I think I am," I said. "I have lots of help," I added. "Nearly an entire magazine staff!"

As Mr. Adams and the others moved on to see the next project, I sat back in my seat and breathed a huge sigh of relief. I had really expected the worst. But in the end, it was the best!

And Mr. Adams didn't think I was a total failure. Though I had to disagree with him about one thing: How hard could it be to host a 'Zine?

I mean, really?

Chapter 6

And the Hits Just Keep on Coming

For the second day in a row I raced up to my bedroom after school to find my mother on my computer.

"Mom!" I cried.

"I know, I know!" my mother replied. "I'm just finishing up! Sorry, honey, but my computer is still down."

I was so anxious to check out my 'Zine and read the ten comments. I had waited patiently all day already. I guess a few more minutes wouldn't kill me. I fell on my bed and listened as my mother worked. Why couldn't she use Miss O's computer? I wondered.

"Don't you have homework?" she asked.

"Yes," I replied. "But I really want to check my 'Zine. I showed it to the class today," I went on, "and I had twenty-one hits and ten comments!"

"Wow, honey, that's incredible!" Mom said, looking up from the screen. "And you have to answer all of them?"

I nodded. "Yup. That's why I really need to get cracking. Please? Mom? Can you hurry up?"

"Sure." She saved her work, and then logged off her account. "It's all yours again," she said. She collected her things and headed toward the door.

"One thing, Juliette," she said before she left.

"What, Mom?"

"I know this project is very important to you," she said. "But I don't want to see that you've neglected your other schoolwork because of it."

"Okay, Mom."

"Really, Juliette. You've committed to a very time-consuming project. Don't get me wrong, I'm proud of you," she added. "But you have to keep on top of your other classes."

"I know. I promise. I will. The girls are going to help me with the 'Zine," I added. Justine, Harlie, and Isabella were coming over in a little while, after Isabella's basketball practice.

Mom smiled. "Great," she said.

After Mom left, I couldn't help but wonder why she and Mr. Adams were so worried about how much work the 'Zine would be. As far as I was concerned, they were worrying about nothing. I had it all under control.

I signed online, then went directly to my 'Zine. This was really so exciting! Can you imagine? Twenty-one hits!

This time, when my home page loaded, I scrolled down to the comments section to check out some of the ten posted comments. I was dying to see what kids at Sage had thought about my first blog article.

I nearly choked when I saw the number of comments was now thirty-three.

"Holy cow!" I cried out loud to myself.

I couldn't believe it. The number had more than tripled since this morning! Dad . . . Mom . . . Mr. Adams . . . they were all right. I was never going to be able to read through all those comments.

I scrolled down further to check the hits counter and I gasped.

00095

I gulped.

Then I suddenly remembered my advice column: "Juliette 9-1-1" I'd completely forgotten to check if anybody had posted for advice. Without a moment to waste, I clicked the "Juliette 9-1-1" link. And all I could do was gawk in amazement at the number of problems that had been posted for me to solve.

44.

I was *doomed*.

Later that afternoon, after Miss O and the girls had returned from Isabella's basketball game, we were seated around the dining room table with Dad's laptop. I had printed out all the " Juliette 9-1-1" problems and all the blog comments and divided them into five groups.

"Okay, everybody! Listen up!" I instructed.

The girls stopped chatting and gave me their attention. I gathered my long hair into a ponytail, then pulled a scrunchie off Miss O's wrist to tie it up with. I was in work-mode . . . and I meant business.

"I know there's a lot here," I told them. "But—"

"Holy moley," Harlie muttered as she skimmed through her papers.

"Yes," I agreed. "Holy moley. Big time holy moley. But I've decided that we can't possibly respond to every single problem and comment."

Miss O laughed out loud. "Not if we want to eat dinner tonight . . . or have a life ever again," she joked.

"Exactly," I said. "It would take forever. So here's the new plan. Every Sunday night I'm going to read through all the new comments and advice problems and pick five of each to respond to. But I need help reading through them all to find the best ones.

"So just go through the pile I gave you and circle the best comments—the funniest, the most interesting, whatever. As for the advice questions, circle the juiciest. Okay?"

The girls nodded.

"What about dinner?" Harlie asked.

I made a face at her. "Is that all you can think about at a time like this?" I asked her. "Your stomach?"

"Yup!" Harlie replied with a grin. "I can't help it if I'm always hungry!" she added. "Plus, I missed snack today because we watched Isabella's practice."

"I offered you half of my cupcake," Miss O reminded her.

"But ew, it was strawberry!" Harlie replied.

I shook my head. "Can we just get to work?" I pleaded. "I'm freaking out here, guys! I mean, as we are sitting here talking about strawberry cupcakes, my 'Zine is getting another hundred or so hits."

"Sorry, Juliette," Harlie said. "But I *am* hungry."

"Mom's making us dinner," I explained.

Harlie grinned. "Yea!" she cheered quietly.

"What is she making?" Justine asked.

I put my head down on the table.

"Hamburgers," Miss O told her. "And veggie burgers for Harlie."

"Okay. Good," Justine said. "Because I had pizza three times in a row and I don't think I could eat it again."

"That's funny," Isabella chimed in. "Because I had pizza *two* nights in a row! First, my parents took me to that Italian restaurant—"

"Hello?!?" I called out, interrupting their conversation. "Working here!"

"Oops. Sorry, Juliette," Isabella said meekly.

"Yeah, sorry!" the others chimed in.

"Can we just do this?" I asked.

The girls all nodded.

"Okay, so start reading!" I instructed.

Everyone glanced down at his or her papers, including me. I had given myself most of the work to do, since, obviously, this was my school project. And thankfully, I noticed, many of the comments were similiar. I was getting stuff like:

COMMENTS: HEY, COOL 'ZINE! YOU ROCK!

COMMENTS: THIS IS FUN! THANKS FOR DOING THIS!

Of course, there were one or two criticisms.

COMMENTS: THIS IS SO DUMB! GET A LIFE!

(Luckily, there weren't a lot of those.)

A few minutes later, Miss O stood up and pushed away her chair.

"Where are you going?" I asked her in a panic.

Miss O blinked. "Uh, I was just getting some lemonade," she replied slowly.

"But you still have some in your glass!" I pointed out.

"But it's not cold anymore," she protested. "I wanted to get some ice and—"

"Miss O! Come on! We have so much of this to get through today!"

"But—"

I groaned. "Okay! Whatever!" I exclaimed. "Just hurry up! Please?"

Miss O returned from the kitchen with a pitcher of lemonade and a plate of cookies.

"Do you have iced tea?" Harlie asked her as she sat down. "I don't really like lemonade."

I glared at her.

"I'm sorry! But I don't like lemonade!"

"Oh, brother!" I cried. "Look, I'll get it for you! Just keep reading! Please!"

I stormed out of the dining room and made a quick batch of iced tea. I couldn't believe the girls were giving me such a hard time. Didn't they realize how much I had to do for this 'Zine?

Back at the table, I resumed going through my pile. As I was scratching off the advice problems I didn't plan on answering, Justine suddenly piped up.

"Hey!" she said excitedly.

"What?" I replied. "What do you need now, different cookies? Cupcakes? What?"

"Sheesh, Juliette," Justine remarked. "I was just going to tell you I found a good advice problem."

"Oh. Sorry. What is it?"

Justine made a face, then continued. "Well, it's not juicy, exactly, but it's still good. Listen.

"Dear Juliette 9-1-1,' Justine began. "I need help. I can't remember my locker combination. I forget it almost every day. Sometimes I write it down, but then I forget where I wrote it. I hate going to the office every single day to get it from them. How can I remember it? It's signed, lovespuppies201."

"Miss O, is that from you?" Isabella asked with a sly smile.

"No!" Miss O replied in a flash. "It's not!"

"Are you sure?" Harlie asked my sister.

"Hey! Come on! I don't even have a locker!" she insisted. "Just a gym locker. And I only forgot my gym locker combination, like, once or twice!"

"Seven times," Harlie corrected.

"Ha-ha," Miss O said dryly. "No way."

"Yup. Seven times," Harlie repeated. "I keep count."

"You do?" Justine asked.

Harlie shook her head. "No. I'm just kidding about the list. But she *does* forget it a lot."

"And she loves puppies!" Isabella chimed in.

"Very funny, you guys," Miss O muttered. "But that letter is not from me. That's not even my screen name."

"We're just messing with you, Miss O," Harlie told her.

"Well, what do you think, Juliette?" Justine asked me. "Is this a good question?"

"Definitely!" I replied. "And here's my advice. I'm going to tell her—or him—to get one of those small, sticky note pads and write her combination on every single sheet. Then she can give the whole pad to her bus driver. Every morning, when she gets off the bus at school, the bus driver can give her one to stick to her shirt so she'll have it when she gets to her locker."

"It's great, Juliette," Miss O remarked.

"Yeah, it's really a good idea," Justine agreed.

"*You* should do that, Miss O," Harlie suggested. "The Post-it notes thing. For gym."

Miss O stuck her tongue out at Harlie. "Ha-ha," she said. "But I don't take the bus," she reminded her. "So who would I give the Post-its to?"

"You could give them to me," Isabella suggested. "Then, every morning, when we meet to walk to school, I could—"

"Guys!" I cried. "Come on! We're wasting time again!"

Miss O made a face at me. Then she went back to her list and her eyes suddenly lit up. "Hey! I have one, too, Juliette," she said. "A good question, I mean."

"Okay, what is it?" I asked.

Miss O cleared her throat. "Dear Juliette 9-1-1. I have a serious problem. My best friend wants to cheat off of me all the time. I don't know what to do about it because she is my very best friend. Should I let her? This one is from someone called 'hoopstar.'"

"Wow, that's a juicy problem, for sure!" Harlie declared. "Don't you think?"

"Absolutely," I agreed. "And it's a tough one, too. I'll use it."

"But how are you going to answer that person?" Isabella asked.

I thought about it for a moment. "Well, I think I will tell him or her to

talk to their best friend. Tell him to tell his friend that he really wants to help him, but cheating is just too dangerous."

"That's good advice," Harlie remarked.

"And maybe I'll tell him to ask his best friend if they can study together for tests instead. This way, the best friend won't need to cheat!" I added.

Isabella grinned. "Great advice! As usual!" she declared.

We had four of our five replies for "Juliette: 9-1-1," when the doorbell rang a short time later. To my surprise, it was Mrs. Brooks, Dana, and Tyler.

"Hey! We're in here! Come on in!" I called to Dana and Tyler when I heard our moms talking in the foyer. Dana came into the dining room with Tyler close behind.

"What are you guys doing?" Dana asked.

"We're going through all the comments and questions that kids submitted to Juliette's 'Zine," Miss O explained.

"Did you see my 'Zine, Tyler?" I asked. He had helped me so much with it the other day, I'd really hoped he'd had a chance to see it. He knew so much about 'Zines and stuff, I valued his opinion.

"Yeah!" he replied. His voice cracked a little as he spoke. "It was so great! Um, I mean, it was really good. Your 'Zine was really good," he said.

I smiled. "Thanks, Tyler!"

His face turned red. "Well, um, do you need any more help?" he asked.

"Definitely!" I told him. "Grab a seat, we're reading through all the comments and stuff."

"I, uh, I brought you a new font program," he said. "It's really cool and let's you scramble different fonts to create new fonts. I got it at the library, but you can download the program no problem."

"Oh, cool. Thanks, Tyler," I said.

"It's, um, in the car. I'll be right back."

"Sorry my brother is such a dork," Dana said after he'd left.

"No, he's not a dork. He's just shy," I commented. "He's really a nice guy. And very helpful."

"I guess," Dana said with a shrug. "So can I help, too?" she asked.

"Sure!" Miss O said. "We're reading through all the comments Juliette got on her 'Zine."

"My 'Zine got almost one hundred hits today," I explained to Dana. "And now I have to reply to people. I mean, if I don't reply, people won't keep visiting."

"You have to answer them every day?" Dana asked in amazement.

"Not every day," I replied. "But every week. Right now, we're actually almost finished. We need to find one more good problem to solve for my advice column."

"I have a problem," Tyler offered as he came back into the room.

Dana rolled her eyes. "What's your problem? They've taken your favorite show, *Space Geeks: The Final Frontier*, off the air?"

"Ha, ha," Tyler said. "Um, anyway, I thought I put the font program in my backpack, but I can't find it. Can I bring it to you tomorrow?" he asked.

"Sure," I told him. "Now grab a pile of printouts and help me find a good problem for the advice column."

"Yeah. Okay." He scanned some of the printouts. "Nobody wrote in with problems with schoolwork or tests? Nothing like that?" he asked hopefully.

I tried not to laugh. "Uh, no, Tyler," I replied. "It's more of an advice column for life problems."

"Oh. Then, um, what about this one?" he asked. He placed a sheet of paper on the top of the pile and began to read.

"Dear Juliette 9-1-1. My teacher hates me. What should I do? It's from anonymous."

Dana rolled her eyes. "*Sheesh!* Tyler, you call that a problem? Juliette wants juicy problems, not lame ones."

"Dana, really, it's okay," I said. "I kind of liked that letter anyway," I said. "I think I want to use it."

"Yeah, it's a good one," Miss O agreed.

Justine, Harlie, and Isabella all nodded.

"Whatever," Dana said. "I'm going to find Mom, anyway," she said. "I really need to get home and study."

Dana and Tyler left a little while later.

"So how are you going to answer that letter Tyler found?" Isabella asked.

I tapped my pen to my chin and thought. "I'm not sure," I said.

"Tell the person that they should bring their teacher a present every day, so that the teacher will like them," Harlie suggested.

"No, that's not a good idea," I told her.

Harlie sighed. "Then tell them to switch classes," she offered.

"No, that's not a good idea either."

"Maybe we can go up to your room for a while, Miss O?" Harlie asked.

I gazed at her in confusion. "Harlie, I didn't mean to say that your ideas were not good," I told her. "It's just that they aren't exactly what I would say."

"I know, I know," Harlie said. She sounded a little hurt, I thought. "I'm just getting kind of bored doing this. And I really wanted to see Miss O's music library before it's time to go home."

"But we aren't finished," I said anxiously.

Miss O cleared her throat. "Uh, Juliette," she said hesitantly, "we helped you for a long time already. We want to just go and hang a bit."

I sighed. I couldn't believe my friends were ditching me in this time of crisis!

"Whatever," I said with a shrug.

The girls followed Miss O out of the dining room and they headed upstairs.

Just then, something written on one of my printouts caught my eye. It was a comment about my blog, and it was written by somebody called "GreenDayFAN."

I read the comment.

COMMENTS: AWESOME 'ZINE! GREAT BLOG. I AGREE WITH YOU, JUJE. IT IS IMPORTANT TO LOOK THE PART IF YOU WANT TO BE AN AMERICAN IDOL. BUT IF YOU DON'T HAVE THE TALENT TO BACK IT UP, THEN YOU ARE NOT THE "TOTAL PACKAGE."

POSTED BY: GREENDAYFAN

I gasped. "Omigod!" I cried up to them. They were just heading up the stairs and stopped to gaze down at me.

"What?" Miss O asked. "What is it?"

My eyes grew wide and I felt my heart thumping in my chest. "I . . . I think this comment here is from Noah!"

"Shut up! No way!" Miss O said. She and the others flew back down the stairs and crowded behind me to read over my shoulder. "Which one?"

I pointed to the comment and Miss O read it out loud.

"What makes you think it's from Noah?" Harlie asked when she'd finished. "It's signed GreenDayFAN. I think there are a lot of people who like Green Day at Sage," she pointed out.

"But how many of them call me Juje?" I asked.

Harlie thought for a minute. "Hmmmm. Good point," she agreed. "But since when does Noah call you Juje?"

"Ever since Miss O called me Juje that morning by the locker," I explained. "Well, he doesn't call me that all the time, but sometimes he does. And he knows I love Green Day. *And,*" I added, "he said 'total package!' That's what he said in school the other day! It's *got* to be him!"

"Then why didn't he post his name?" Miss O asked. "A lot of people posted their names in their comments."

"Maybe he figured I'd know it was him?" I guessed.

The others shrugged.

"Well, I think it's definitely him," I stated.

"So you're still crushing on Noah Sclar?" Justine asked with a smile.

I sighed, then shook my head. "No, not really," I replied. "Well, maybe a *little*," I confided. "But not a full-blown crush. Oh, I don't know!"

"Are you going to write him back this weekend?" Harlie asked.

I nodded. "Yup! But not this weekend. I'm going to write back right now and put in another blog for tomorrow!"

"Are you sure, Juliette?" Miss O asked. "I thought you were only going to put in a new blog once a week."

"I was," I told her. "But I really want to reply to Noah."

"Sheesh! I thought you said you were behind schedule and that we were wasting time and blah, blah, blah! Is there really enough time to write

a new blog and all the answers for the advice column?" Miss O asked. "*And* do the other updates to the 'Zine?"

I groaned. Right. I still had to do all that.

Mom piped her head in just then. "Dinner's just about ready, girls!" she announced. "And after dinner, I'll give you all a ride home."

"Okay, let's move this all into the family room," I said, neatly stacking the printouts and logging off Dad's laptop. I looked pleadingly at my BFFs. "Listen, can you do this for me?" I begged. "Answer that last advice problem and move all this stuff for me? I want to run upstairs and write back to Noah before dinner. If I do, maybe he'll see it and write me back again tonight!"

"Um, but Juliette," Miss O started. "We were just—"

"Please, oh please?" I begged her.

"I thought you said my advice was lame," Harlie remarked.

"I didn't mean that!" I insisted. "It's good. It's great! Whatever you answer will be fine with me. Please?"

Miss O finally nodded. "Yeah, okay," she said.

"Yeah, go ahead," Harlie added. "We'll finish this up for you."

"Thanks, guys!" I told them. "You rock! I'll be back in a sec! I promise!"

"Oh, no," I heard Harlie say really loudly in the dinning room as I raced up the steps to my room. "She does *not* have a crush on Noah Sclar! No way! No crushes going on here!"

"Ha-ha. I heard that!" I called back downstairs.

But as the words left my mouth, I thought to myself: Who was I kidding? My crush on Noah was now most definitely full-blown.

Chapter 7

Just When Everything Was Perfect

The next day, as I headed to the cafeteria for lunch, I mentally replayed what had happened in Computer Clicks class earlier that morning. It wasn't anything super-serious, but it had me wondering: Had Noah posted that comment in my 'Zine, or not? I mean, I'd written back to his comment last night, but he hadn't written back again. And in class this morning, he hadn't even hinted that he was GreenDayFAN.

Here's what happened:

When I'd arrived to class, Noah was already on the computer.

"Hey," I'd said. "How's it going?" I'd been dying to bring up the posting from the night before, but if I did, and he wasn't the one who'd written it, I'd feel like a Class A Jerk.

Noah hadn't even looked up from the screen. "Okay," he mumbled. "Just a sec, I'm really busy, Juliette."

Hmmm.

"Oh, no problem," I'd said. "I just have to check if there were any more posts on my 'Zine." Then I sat back and waited for him to mention my 'Zine.

"Hey, I read your blog, you know," he then said.

"You did?" I asked. *Awesome!*

"Yeah, where you wrote about looking like an American Idol? I couldn't believe how many people wrote comments."

"Yes. Well—"

"And how stupid some of them were!" he'd interrupted me. "Like all those people who think you can still become a big star if you don't have 'the look,' you know what I mean? How dumb is that? The "look" is the most important thing! You have to look like an idol to become one."

Huh?

I'd had no idea what to say. That was totally opposite of what he'd written in the comment yesterday! *Unless, he hadn't written that comment at all!*

It was all so confusing!

That's why now, walking toward the cafeteria, I couldn't stop thinking about what Noah had said and that posted comment from yesterday. I had been so sure he was the one who wrote it! I mean, who *else* likes Green Day *and* calls me Juje?

But there was one major difference: Noah and I totally disagreed on what it meant to be a pop star. He'd made that obvious in class this morning. So was he the writer, or not? I wondered. And more importantly, was he interested in me . . . or not?

I couldn't be sure of anything at that point.

I stepped into the cafeteria and headed toward the table where I usually sat, with some of my neighborhood friends. Sometimes I liked to go over to the other cafeteria to sit with Miss O and the girls, but today I didn't think I had enough time.

I walked past Noah's table, trying not to look like I was checking him out (when I really was!) and to my surprise, he called out to me.

"Yo! Juje! Grab a chair!" he said.

What?

I was completely caught off guard.

"Um, yeah, okay!" I said. To my relief, Noah sat at a table that had girls, too. He sat with his two best friends, Declan Petit and Connor West, and Connor's cousins, Heather and Amanda Epstein. Heather and Amanda were sisters and Heather was in my grade. I was in a few classes with her and she was super nice.

I dropped my stuff on the table, taking the seat across from Noah and next to Heather.

"We were just talking about Sage Sings," Noah explained. Sage Sings was the name of the "Battle of the Bands" music night at our school. It was held every year, for grades five through twelve.

"Cool," I said. "I think it's going to be great this year," I added. "I heard some of the teachers are forming a band and they are going to perform, too."

"Get out!" Heather cried. "That is so awesome! Which teachers?"

"And what kind of music do they play?" Amanda wanted to know.

"I only know three of the teachers for sure," I told them all. "Mr.

Feuerzeig from lower division, and Ms. Schultz and Mr. McPartlan from middle. Oh, and I think Principal Sack!"

The kids at the table laughed. It was funny to picture Principal Sack playing in a rock band.

"And they play beach music," I added. "I'm not exactly sure what that means."

"We don't play that kind of music," Noah said, referring to his band, As If. "We play pop and rock, mostly."

"Are you going to Sage Sings, Juliette?" Heather asked.

"Definitely!" I replied. "I wouldn't miss it! It's, like, the most fun night of the year."

The others agreed.

"Are you going to write about it in your 'Zine?" Noah wanted to know.

I shrugged. "Yeah, I guess," I said.

"Your 'Zine is so cool!" Amanda gushed.

"Yeah, everybody is talking about it!" Heather added. "You're famous!"

I felt my face turn red. "Thanks," I managed to say. "But I'm not exactly famous."

"Well, we all love it," Amanda told me. "I check it every night before I log off," she added. "And I posted something last night. About Sage Sings. Did you read it?"

"Well, I try to read all the comments," I told her. "But there are too many. So my sister and her friends all help."

"It wasn't anything monumental," she said. "I think I wrote, 'Sage Rocks!' or something like that! You know, for school spirit."

"Gonna use that school spirit to vote for As If at Sage Sings?" Noah asked her.

"Hmmm, I don't know," Amanda joked. "I mean Principal Sack can really get funky!"

Everybody laughed.

"Ooooh, and don't you just love when they have a deejay at the end of the night?" Heather asked. "No offense, Noah," she added, "you know I *love* As If concerts! But I also love the hip hop music and all the dancing with the deejay."

"And the give-aways!" Amanda piped in. "Last year, the Sage Sings deejay gave out glow-in-the-dark rope, remember? We made bracelets and stuff?"

"Yeah, that was fun," I remembered. It *had* been a total blast last year. As a fifth grader it was the first year I was able to go. This year, Miss O, Isabella, Justine, and Harlie would be invited, too.

"As If is going to rock this year," Noah said confidently. "Any songs you girls want to request?"

"Really?" I asked.

"Yeah," he said. "We play everything. Everything *cool*, that is. What's your favorite song? Something by Green Day?"

"Well, I do *love* Green Day," I said.

Before I could think of a song suggestion, somebody tapped me on the shoulder. I spun around to find Tyler, holding an armload of books and trying to balance his lunch tray at the same time.

"Oh! Hey, Tyler!" I said.

He cleared his throat. "Uh, I have another idea for your 'Zine," he blurted out, without even saying, "Hey! Hi! Or, How ya doing?"

"Oh, um, great!" I said awkwardly. It was just so weird of him to come over and start talking to me like that. "But can we talk about it later?" I asked. "I'll give you a call after school."

I barely heard his reply because he spun around so quickly and walked away before the words were even out of my mouth! OMG, he could be so weird sometimes! When I turned back to the table, I saw Heather roll her eyes.

"What is wrong with him?" she asked bluntly.

"He's uh, not so bad," I said. "He's actually a really nice guy."

"Maybe in outer space," Noah laughed.

The others laughed, too.

"Uh, no, really. I've known him since forever," I told them. "Our dads work together. He just gets nervous around groups of people." I was feeling really uncomfortable talking about Tyler this way. Why did I feel compelled to stand up for him like that?

"You mean nervous around *humans*," Noah joked again.

Again, everyone at the table cracked up. I didn't know what to do, so I joined them and chuckled, too. Truth? I felt horrible about it. Really horrible. But I had been totally clicking with these guys ever since I sat down. I was having so much fun at Noah's table. I didn't want to ruin it!

So I laughed . . . but in my heart of hearts I knew it was the wrong thing to do. I felt so bad, I made a mental note to call Tyler later that evening and listen to his 'Zine idea.

At home that afternoon, I sat on the floor of my bedroom with about a trillion printouts in piles all around me. The hits counter on my 'Zine was now over six hundred, and I think every single kid at Sage School had sent me a problem to solve! (Did I mention that I had math homework and a spelling test tomorrow, too?)

Downstairs in the kitchen I could hear Miss O and Isabella hanging out. They seemed to be having a lot of fun—Miss O was testing a new recipe for her next 'Zine column (pita pizzas, I think?) and Isabella was helping her grate mozzarella cheese. I would have liked to join them, but that was impossible. There was so much work still to be done!

Suddenly, I remembered Tyler. I grabbed my cell phone and dialed his number.

"Oh, hi, Dana," I said when she answered the phone. "Can I speak to Tyler?"

"How come?" Dana asked right away.

Boy, talk about nosy!

"Nothing, really. I just wanted to talk to him about my next blog. He said he had a good idea for me."

"Well, he's not here," she replied. "He's out with Dad at some writing thing."

That got my attention.

"What writing thing?" I asked.

"Oh, it's just some dumb writing workshop at Westchester U.," she replied. "It's stupid, I don't know. So anyway, how's your 'Zine coming along?"

I wondered what writing workshop was at the University . . . and how come *I'd* never heard about it before? I would have *loved* to be in a writing workshop class!

"It's coming," I replied. "Listen, can you tell Tyler to call me when he gets home?" I asked.

"Yeah, I'll tell dork-o you called," she said.

She hung up and at the same time I snapped my cell shut, I heard the girls burst out laughing downstairs. Normally, I would have raced downstairs to ask them to fill me in on the joke, but today I was too swamped. I couldn't believe how much I had to do! And I had to secretly admit I was a little mad at Miss O and Isabella for not offering to come upstairs and help me.

Back in front of my computer screen, I scrolled through the newest advice questions. I wanted to load the responses to the ones we picked yesterday onto the host site to be ready to launch in Monday's new issue. As I was scrolling, Miss O called to me from downstairs.

"Juliette!" she shouted.

"Coming!" I yelled back. I got up from my chair, and headed for the top of the stairs. "What is it, Miss O?" I called down. I could smell something yummy cooking—I think it *was* her famous pita pizzas. They were famous because she always made them with lots of different types of cheeses.

"Tyler and his father are here!" Miss O called up to me.

"Really? That's funny!" I said. "I just called Tyler!"

I went downstairs and found Tyler in the kitchen with Miss O and Isabella.

"Tyler, I just called you!" I said with a grin. "Just a second ago. I spoke to Dana."

"I was, um, out," Tyler said. "I have a writing workshop at Westchester University once a week after school," he explained.

"She told me," I said. "And I'm so jealous!"

Tyler's blushed. "You are? Why?" he asked.

"Omigod, because I *love* to write!" I told him. "I want to be a writer someday."

"Oh. Me, too," he said. "That's actually what my idea for your 'Zine was about."

My eyes widened. "Tell!" I instructed.

Tyler cleared his throat and ran his fingers through his bright blond hair. I decided I really liked how Tyler was wearing his hair these days. He'd gotten one of those cool haircuts with the bangs spiked up in the front. If only he wasn't so completely shy and goofy all the time, I thought, he'd be a total dude.

"Okay," he began, "what if you asked people to send in their stories or poems or something they wrote and you could, like, judge them every week and post the best one?" He gazed hopefully at me. "I could help you, if you want."

Miss O, who'd been listening, interrupted. "Juliette, that's such a great idea!" she said. But I didn't need to hear that from my sister to know that it was true.

Tyler grinned.

"Is that why you came over?" I asked. "To tell me your idea?"

Before Tyler could answer, his father and my mom and dad came into the kitchen. They wore very excited smiles, so I knew something was up.

"We came over to tell you the big surprise!" Mr. Brooks announced.

Me, Tyler and Miss O stared at him in confusion.

"What surprise?" I asked.

Our parents exchanged looks.

"We're going back to Windham Mountain!" my father said cheerfully. "And this time we're all going together, for a whole weekend of skiing and snowboarding!"

"Us, too?" Tyler asked

My dad nodded. "Yup! Both families. And we're staying at the Moose Lodge!"

Miss O and I jumped up and down with excitement. How cool was that? I thought. We'd had so much fun at Windham Mountain a few weeks ago. And Moose Lodge was awesome! It had an indoor pool and really cool activities like scavenger hunts and karaoke contests.

Not to mention the best hot cocoa in New York.

"Dad, that is so excellent!" I cried. "Can I take snowboarding lessons?" I asked. "Please?"

My father nodded. Then he pointed to Tyler. "Tyler is an expert level boarder," he told me. "You may want him to give you lessons."

I spun around to Tyler. "Really?" I asked. "You board?"

Tyler nodded shyly. "Uh, yeah," he said.

"He's just being modest!" his father gushed. "Tyler won a medal at Stratton Mountain last year."

I stared at Tyler in disbelief. Who would have known?

"Can you give me snowboard lessons then?" I asked.

"And me, too?" Miss O asked.

"Yeah, sure," he said, smiling.

Miss O and I continued to dance around in excitement. "This is so perfect! I can't wait!" I cried.

"You don't have to wait, honey!" my mother said. "That's the best part—we were able to get reservations for *this* weekend!"

I was just about to shout, "*Woo-hoo!*" when it hit me, as the expression goes, like a ton of bricks.

This weekend?

The same weekend as Sage Sings?

Oh, no!

Chapter 8

Letters and Lies

It's no use, I thought miserably, lying in bed, staring at the ceiling. *No way were Mom and Dad going to change their minds. We were headed for Windham this weekend, "and that was that!" as Dad had just said.*

I groaned and flipped onto my stomach, resting my chin on the tops of my hands. How had things gone from super-great to super-horrible in such a short time? An hour ago I was planning what I would wear Saturday night for Sage Sings, and now I was planning on how to tell Noah I would not be there after all.

Miss O knocked on my door. "Juliette?" she called out.

"Yeah?"

"Can I come in?" she asked.

"Uh-huh."

Miss O had just showered and was already dressed in her pj's, or, what she likes to wear to sleep every night: an extra, extra, extra large T-shirt. The one she had on tonight was from a soccer cup tournament from last fall. She plopped down on the edge of my bed and began brushing out her damp hair. "Are you okay?" she asked.

"I guess," I muttered. I suppose she was worried because I had sounded very "not okay" a little while ago when I was fighting with Mom and Dad about changing the weekend of the ski trip.

"Come on, Juje. Don't be so upset. It'll be fun!" she said, trying her best to convince me. "Moose Lodge! We always said how cool it would be to stay there!"

"I know, I know," I said glumly. "I know it'll be tons of fun. But I just don't understand why it has to be *this* weekend."

"Hey, I'm missing Sage Sings, too," she pointed out. "And it would have been my first year," she added. "But there will be other Sage Sings."

I flipped back over onto my back. "I know," I said again. "It's just that I really, *really* wanted to see As If this weekend. I already told Noah I was going!"

"So tell him you're going snowboarding," Miss O suggested. "Guys love snowboarding. He'll think that's a way cool excuse!"

I managed a laugh. "Maybe," I said.

Miss O got up from my bed. "Okay. I have to work on a poster for my science class project," she said, making a face. "It's due Monday, but now that we're going away all weekend, I need to finish it. But come in if you need to talk," she added. "And, I promise, we're going to have so much fun learning to board, you'll forget all about Noah and As If!"

"Yeah, sure. *As if*," I muttered, trying to make a lame joke.

After Miss O left, I got out of bed and sat down at the computer. I logged onto my host page for the 'Zine. I had to get started on a new blog—especially that I was now going to be away all weekend. I wanted to write about the creative writing contest idea Tyler had suggested. I decided to call the contest: "Creative Sages."

The blog took a few minutes to write. It was really a lot like writing in a diary or a journal. The big difference was everyone in the world could read an Internet blog. Nobody but *you* can read your diary!

When I finished blogging, I grabbed my bathrobe and headed for the shower. I was so excited to see Mom had bought new shampoo for Miss O and me. My favorite kind, too. The shampoo that smells like cake. It's so amazing and crazy that it really does smell exactly like freshly baked cake.

Anyway, as I was shampooing, the funniest thing happened. I started writing a poem in my head! It was weird because I never make up poems and stuff while I'm in the shower. Mostly, I just like to sing or pretend I'm auditioning for *American Idol*. (That is, until Miss O bangs on the bathroom door and tells me I'll never be Kelly Clarkson.) But I guess after feeling so moody and bummed all night, I had all these emotions bottled up inside me. So instead of singing, I "wrote!" By the time I finished my shower, I had written a poem to enter in my own creative writing contest!

Well, actually I couldn't enter my own contest (mostly because I was the contest judge, too!). But I thought it would be great to post my new poem along with the blog I'd just written about the contest. Then kids could get an idea of what sort of things they could write about to enter.

Anyway, I threw on my bathrobe and wrapped my hair up in a towel. (Miss O always brushes out her hair after the shower, then lets it dry

naturally, but I always let it dry in a towel first, then I style it with a hair dryer and diffuser.)

Back in my room, I sat down at my computer. I was about to post the poem, but decided that before I put it out there for the whole world to see, I first needed some feedback. So I shot off an e-mail to the girls to see what they thought.

To: g0algirl, JUSTme713, harliegirl95, izzyBELLA
From: jujuBEE
Subject: Check out a Love Poem by ME

Yo, girlfriends! I wrote this poem just now (in the shower!!!) and I want to put it in my 'Zine. First tell me what y'all think. Is it way sappy? Dumb? Dopey?. . . Amazing???

lemme know. . . Juje

R U Thinking of Me?
If I'm not there
Do you care?
When I'm not with you
I keep wishing I were.
24/7, it's always in my brain.
But are you doing the same,
Or to you is this a game?

R U Thinking of Me,
When all I can do
Is think about U?

I hit "send," then glanced at the time on my computer screen. It was only seven p.m., so hopefully, the girls would get a chance to read it and write back to me before they went to bed for the night. I noticed on my Buddy List that everyone was online, so maybe they would read it soon.

In the meantime, I got back to work. First, I checked on my Juliette 9-1-1 column. Four more problems were posted since the last time I checked.

I clicked on the first one and read the letter. This is what it said:

Dear Juliette 9-1-1,

I have a friend who is totally OOC (Out Of Control)! She has become way bossy and demanding and she's ruining our friendship!!! Like for instance, she is doing this thing for school and it is taking over her entire life. It is all she talks about. My friends and I offered to help her just to be nice (and because we thought it would be fun). But it's not fun at all! All she does is work us to death and tell us our ideas are lame.

Any advice???

From, Tired of Being Bossed

As I waited for my friends to e-mail me back, I started to answer the letter. I felt so bad for this person because I normally can't stand bossy people. Like Dana for instance—she can be pretty bossy sometimes.

Dear Tired of Being Bossed,

I know exactly what you need to do. You need to tell your friend she is acting bossy! Tell her right away, before she really does get out of control! Tell her you love her lots, but you hate being told what to do. Remind her that you offered to help her out and that she needs to just chill and accept the help.

Juliette 9-1-1.

Miss O came into my room just as I was saving the reply in my 'Zine file. From the corner of my eye I saw my e-mail link flashing: I had e-mail waiting for me. I clicked it and found that I had four messages. The girls had all gotten back to me!

"One is from me," Miss O said, reading over my shoulder.

To: jujuBEE

From: harliegirl95

Subject: Re: Check out a Love Poem by ME

YES! Gr8 poem! Go for it!

To: jujuBEE

From: JUSTme713

Subject: Re: Check out a Love Poem by ME

Really nice poem, J. I really liked it.

-Justine

To: jujuBEE
From: IzzyBELLA
Subject: RE: Check out a Love Poem by ME

Is this about you and Noah??? Anyway, I loved it!

To: jujuBEE
From: g0algirl
Subject: RE: Check out a Love Poem by ME

Hey, Juje...excellent poem! You should think about becoming a writer. . . ;)
-miss o

After reading what they'd said, I felt better about posting my poem in the 'Zine. My BFFs would never lie to me and tell me it was good when it wasn't. So I copied it from my file, chose a really cool font, then posted it next to my blog. My hope was that other kids would read my blog about the Creative Sages writing contest, then, if they didn't know what to write, they could read my poem to get an example of something good to write about.

Before I went to bed for the night, I read through as many more comments as I could. Tomorrow was Thursday, which meant the girls were coming over after Miss O's soccer practice to help me with next week's 'Zine. And we had to work extra hard and extra fast tomorrow,

because now that I was going away for the weekend, I was going to need to have it all finished *before* we left for Windham on Friday night!

Was that even possible? I wondered.

Honestly, Mr. Adams, Dad, Mom—they had all been right about the amount of work involved with this project. I should have listened. Maintaining an online magazine was no small potatoes!

An hour later, I was *still* reading through the comments. There was a knock on my door and my dad stuck his hand in my room and waved a small flag. It was funny.

"Are we okay?" he asked, leaning into my room.

I managed a laugh. "Yeah," I said. "Sorry about going all dramatic earlier," I said.

"And I'm sorry for springing these plans on you and your sister," Dad said. "But we had to act fast to get the room at Moose Lodge. I didn't realize you had your school concert this weekend."

"So can I stay home?" I asked, gazing up at him hopefully.

"Ha!" he replied. "What do you think?"

I made a face. "Not in a million years, right?"

"Right." Dad kissed the top of my head and left the room. Then he poked back inside.

"I almost forgot," he said. "I can take you to your tennis match tomorrow, if you'd like. My late meeting got cancelled."

My stomach lurched. *Tennis match? Tomorrow night?*

"I totally forgot I had a match tomorrow night!" I cried.

"It's your last in this tournament," Dad reminded me.

"What am I going to do?" I fretted. "I have to finish my 'Zine tomorrow night because we're going away! How am I going to do that *and* play in the match?"

My father looked at my sympathetically. "I wish I could tell you what to do," he said. "But it's your decision. Can't you just leave the 'Zine for a week?"

I gazed at my computer screen, and at all the comments that still needed to be read, the problems that needed solving, while I thought about all the new recipes, sports news and comic strips I'd promised to post each week.

Amanda Epstein's words rang in my mind: "Everyone loves your 'Zine! You're famous!"

And Heather's, "I check it every night before I log off!"

And all the kids who wrote in asking for advice—could I leave them hanging like that?

Then, of course, there was Noah. What if he really *had* been the one to post that letter, I wondered. How could I just let it all go, and not reply to anyone for a whole week? No way. I couldn't do that!

My heart was beating heavily in my chest.

What had I gotten myself into?

The next morning, I woke up late and didn't have a chance to check my 'Zine before leaving for school. I'd stayed up late devising a plan that would allow me to get everything done tomorrow despite my tennis match. My plan included skipping lunch in the cafeteria that day, again, and instead, bringing a bag lunch to the computer lab so I could work on my 'Zine.

“Maybe you guys can come, too?” I asked my sister and friends that morning as we hung out by the “doorz” waiting for school to begin.

To my surprise, no one said anything.

“Uh, hello?” I said. “How about it? Can you meet me at the computer lab today?”

Finally Isabella agreed. “Yeah, sure, Juliette. I’ll meet you.”

“Thanks! So it’ll be me, you, Miss O—” I began.

“Actually, Juliette,” Miss O interrupted, “I don’t think I can help you during lunch today. I have some stuff to do.”

I gazed at her in disbelief. “What stuff?” I asked. “Come on—I’m counting on you! Since we’re going skiing this weekend, I need to get everything done before we leave!”

“I don’t think I can, Juliette,” Miss O said hesitantly. “I, um, have a lot of school work, too.”

“But I need your new recipe, Harlie’s next comic, Isabella’s sports news, some more pictures and interviews from Justine . . . I need all of it!” I insisted. “I won’t be able to do any work on my ’Zine at Moose Lodge, that’s for sure! What am I going to do?”

“Can’t you just skip a week?” Harlie asked.

I groaned. Nobody understood the pressure I was under to get a new ’Zine out every week. I mean, kids were logging on every day to read it! And there were so many problems to solve! How could I possibly let all those people down?

“Maybe you can finish it when we get back from Windham on Sunday?” Miss O offered.

“You guys are so lucky!” Harlie chimed in. “Moose Lodge sounds like a blast!”

I didn't answer her, since I was still pretty bummed about having to go away in the first place and miss the school event of the year. Not to mention I was also a little P.O.'d at my sister at that moment for refusing to help me during lunch. "Yeah. I guess," was all I said.

"Juliette!" Harlie cried. "Come on! Get pumped! You're gonna have so much fun!"

"Yeah, stop thinking about missing Sage Sings," Isabella said. "Your ski trip sounds much, much more fun."

I shrugged. "It's just that I told Noah—"

Harlie cleared her throat loudly at the mention of Noah. "You mean Noah, the guy you *don't* have a crush on?" she asked with a sly smile.

"Yes, *that* Noah," I said coolly. "I already told him I wouldn't miss Sage Sings and that I was excited about hearing his band play."

"He'll forgive you, Juliette," Miss O said.

I ignored her. "Anyway, who else is in for computer lab during lunch?" I asked the girls.

"I'll be there," Justine said.

"And me," Harlie added.

"Count us in, too, I guess," Miss O finally relented.

I gave her a huge hug. "Thank you so much," I told her. "Thank all of you! Now I'd better get going," I told them. "I'll see you guys at lunchtime, in the computer lab."

The girls all nodded.

"See you later!"

I ran toward the middle division building and thought about how I would break the news to Noah. As I ran, I heard my cell phone ring inside

my jacket pocket. I pulled out my cell and flipped it open. It was a text message from Dad.

JUJE, STILL MAD? HOPE NOT. HOW 'BOUT WE HIT INDR CRTS THIS WKEND, 2?

I grinned, then punched a text message back to him.

NOT MAD. TENNIS SOUNDS GR8. BUT I WILL KICK UR BUTT!

I could never stay mad at my dad anyway. I knew it, and he knew it. We have an awesome relationship. And truth be told, knowing we were going to spend an hour or two together on the indoor tennis courts at Moose Lodge *did* make me feel a little more pumped about going to Windham!

Back to Noah.

I still had to break the news to him. I'd tell him, I decided, that the ski trip was a family obligation and that I *had* to go. That I felt awful about it, but that I had no choice.

And in no way, I decided, would I mention that I was going with Tyler Brooks!

As I approached the lockers, I was surprised to see Noah, Declan, and Connor standing around mine. Noah was actually leaning on my locker. My heart leapt a little. Was he waiting for me? I wondered.

"Hey, Juje!" Noah called down the hall when he saw me. "What's up?"

I smiled. "Hi, Noah. Nothing really."

Noah moved out of the way so I could open my locker door. "Listen," he said. "Declan and Connor said you made a really cool poster for your 'Zine last week. With a comic strip character?"

I nodded. "My friend Harlie made it," I told him. "She drew that character herself. Isn't it awesome?"

"Well, I didn't really get a chance to see it," Noah said.

I looked at him strangely. How could he not have seen it? I wondered. The posters were all over school. And wouldn't he have seen Harlie's "Harlie Rox" on my 'Zine, which he said he'd read???

"Are you sure?" I asked. "We put posters up all over. Harlie put her superhero on it, with a little white dog? They're both wearing hot pink and black and—"

Noah shook his head. "Nope," he said vaguely. "But anyway, I wanted to know if you—or your friend—"

"Harlie," I reminded him.

"Yeah, Harlie, could make some cool posters for As If, too. You know, for the Sage Sings concert tomorrow night."

Ugh. Well, there it was. We were already talking about Sage Sings. There was no avoiding my bad news anymore. No way around it now. I had to come clean and tell Noah I wasn't going to be there.

"Noah, about Sage Sings," I began.

Noah's face lit up. "We are so gonna rock!" he said to Declan and Connor. "As If *rules*!"

The guys all high-fived.

"About that," I said again. "I can't make posters for you, Noah," I said. "I'm really sorry, but I can't. And, I have some more bad news."

Noah looked at me. "Huh?" he asked.

Blah! I hated this!

"Um, well, it looks like I can't go to Sage Sings after all," I finally blurted out.

Noah made a face. "How come?" he asked.

I was just about to explain, when I saw Tyler walking toward us.

"Hi!" Tyler said with a grin. "Uh, I saw your 'Zine—" he began.

"Hey, Tyler," I said. "Can we talk later? I'm in the middle of something here."

Tyler's face fell. "Oh. Um, okay," he said. "But, uh, I just wanted to tell you that I went online last night and reserved snowboards for you and Miss O. For this weekend."

Uh-oh.

I could feel Noah staring at me.

"Yeah, okay! That's cool," I said, trying not to show how uncomfortable I was with my weekend plans now wide out in the open. "Thanks. But can we talk later?"

Tyler nodded. "Well, okay," he said. "Um, so, bye. I mean, later."

As soon as he was gone, Noah and his friends burst out laughing.

"Is that right? Are you going away this weekend?" Noah said, trying to catch his breath. "With Tyler Brooks? King of all Dorks?"

I felt my face turn red.

"Uh, that's what I was trying to tell you," I said. "I'll be away this weekend."

"With that space case?" Noah asked.

"I . . . I . . . I have to," I blurted out. "It's a work thing for my father's business," I lied.

"That's horrible," Noah went on. "What a loser. How can you be friends with him?"

"We have to go!" I insisted. "Or . . . or . . . or my father will get fired!"

I have no idea why I lied like that, but once it flew out of my mouth, it was too late to stop it. Of course, it wasn't true at all.

"Bummer," Noah said. "You're going to miss a rockin' concert." He high-fived again with Declan and Connor.

"Yeah, I know," I said, still uneasy from the lies I'd just told.

"Well, I gotta get going," Noah said. "See ya in class." He spun around and began to walk away, still laughing with his friends over my weekend plans with Tyler.

"Okay, see you in class!" I called to him, but I don't think he heard me.

When he had disappeared down the hall, I slumped against my locker and sighed.

That had not gone well at all.

In fact, I think I had managed to screw up, in a matter of minutes, both my relationship with Noah, *and* my friendship with Tyler.

As I stood there, leaning against my new periwinkle-decorated locker, for the first time that year I wished my sister and I were still in the same building. If there was anyone I needed to see right at that very moment, it was Miss O.

Juliette 9-1-1 was in need of some good advice herself.

Chapter 9

The Mysterious Love Song

I was sitting in history class watching the clock when finally, the bell rang. *Lunchtime!*

I practically bolted up from my desk and raced to the computer lab—I just couldn't wait to check my 'Zine . . . and to see my sister and my best friends and fill them in on what had happened with Noah.

Luckily, the computer lab was empty—I was the only one who had signed up to use it during lunch today. I stepped inside and logged onto five computers. Then I made sure the scanner was turned on, too. Harlie was bringing the last part of her comic strip for the new issue of the 'Zine and it needed to be scanned.

When everything was all ready for our lunchtime work meeting, I sat

down at one of the computers and logged onto my 'Zine. To my surprise, twenty-eight more people had already responded to my blog from yesterday!

I clicked on the blog to read the comments. The first one was so nice! Somebody had written to me that they really liked my poem.

COMMENTS: COOL POEM! I THINK YOU ARE A TALENTED WRITER. I WOULD LIKE TO POST SOMETHING, BUT I DON'T KNOW WHAT TO WRITE.

I clicked the next comment.

COMMENTS: HEY! THAT WAS A GR8 POEM!!! I DIDN'T WRITE A POEM, BUT I WROTE A JOKE FOR CREATIVE SAGES. WHAT DID THE TATTERED PIECE OF STRING SAY TO THE OTHER PIECE OF STRING, WHEN IT ASKED HER OUT? I'M A FRAYED KNOT. (I'M AFRAID NOT!) GET IT?

I laughed to myself, even though jokes weren't exactly what I'd had in mind for Creative Sages.

The next comment was posted by somebody called gottagettagotchie:

COMMENTS: MY PET

MY PET IS FAITHFUL, MY PET IS STRONG.

WHEREVER I GO, I TAKE HIM ALONG.

HE'S LITTLE AND CUTE—AS CUTE AS A BUTTON,

ACTUALLY, HE IS AS CUTE AS TWO BUTTONS.

IS IT A KITTY? A PUPPY WHO'S SCRATCHY?

NOPE, IT'S MY VERSION 3 TAMAGOTCHIE.

I let out another laugh. Okay, I thought. Someone is a little too into their electronic pet! Still, I *did* say you could write about *anything*.

Just as I clicked on the next comment, Miss O and the girls flew through the door.

"We're here!" Miss O announced. "So tell! How'd it go this morning? Did you tell Noah about the ski trip?"

I sighed. "Yes, I told him. But it didn't go well at all! Just as I was telling him, Tyler came by and interrupted me. So when Noah heard I was going skiing with Tyler, he and his friends cracked up."

Miss O made a face. "Ouch," she said. "What did you do?"

I bit my bottom lip. "I sort of told a little lie," I explained.

"Why? How come?" Harlie asked.

"I'm still not completely sure," I said with a groan. "I was just so uncomfortable standing there, listening to Noah and his friends diss on Tyler, I just pretended to think it was funny, too."

"I don't get it," Isabella said. "What did you lie about?"

"Well, I kind of told Noah that we *had* to go to skiing this weekend," I said.

"Well, we *do* have to go," Miss O pointed out. "Dad said so."

I nodded. "Right," I agreed. "But, I also told Noah that it was a work thing and that if we didn't go, Dad could get fired."

Miss O's eyes widened. "What?" she cried. "Are you *insane*?"

"I know! It was awful," I confided. "But honestly, it just popped right out of my mouth! Do you know when that happens? When you say something and as you're saying it, you're wondering why you're saying it?"

The girls all nodded.

"Well, that's what happened," I said flatly. "I didn't mean to make it up, but I really didn't want Noah to hate me because I couldn't go to Sage Sings. And I also didn't want him to think Tyler was my new BF."

"Tyler's cool," Justine said. "Well, he's not exactly *cool*, but he's really sweet and he would be so cute if he just chilled out a little."

"No, I know that," I said. "But I didn't want Noah to think I'd rather go skiing with Tyler than see As If. So I pretended to think Tyler was a dork."

The girls were quiet.

"Look, I know it was a rotten thing to do," I said. "And actually, it didn't even work either, because all through Computer Clicks, Noah barely said a word to me."

"Really? That stinks, Juje," Miss O said.

"It definitely does," I told the girls. "Because not only did I maybe mess up things with Noah, but when Tyler interrupted us this morning, I wasn't very friendly to him, either."

"Sheesh, Juliette!" Isabella cried. "Sounds like a pretty lame morning!"

I nodded. "Yeah, it hasn't been such a fabulous day so far," I agreed. "Oh! But wait! Some people responded to my new blog!" I told them. "About the new writing feature. Someone sent me a joke to post. And another person sent me a poem about their toy Tamagotchie."

Harlie narrowed her eyes at me. "Say what?"

I laughed. "I know it sounds strange. But some kid really likes his Tamagotchie and he wrote a poem about it."

"Can we see it?" Isabella asked.

The girls crowded around me and I clicked back to the screen with the poem. Harlie and Isabella thought it was funny, but Justine and Miss O thought it was stupid.

"Well, I *did* say you could write about anything," I told them. "And if your favorite thing is your electronic pet, then so be it."

"What about your advice column?" Miss O asked. "Any good new letters?"

"Not really," I replied.

"None at all?" she asked again. From the corner of my eye I noticed her exchange a look with the girls.

What was *that* about? I wondered.

"No," I said again. "Nothing interesting. Why?"

Miss O shrugged. "No reason," she said. "I was just asking."

Hmmm. Something weird was going on with my sister. I was about to mention it, when Justine interrupted my thoughts.

"What's that?" she asked, pointing to a strange little icon next to one of the blog comments near the bottom. It looked like a teeny, little musical note.

"I don't have a clue," I replied. "Music?" I wondered out loud.

"Click it!" Harlie said. "Let's check it out."

I put the curser over the musical note and clicked. To my surprise, another window opened on the screen and a music playing program began to load.

"Someone posted music?" Justine asked.

"Looks that way," I said. "I wonder what it is?" I couldn't imagine what was posted. I waited patiently for the sound clip to load. Then, all of a sudden, we all heard the soft strumming of a guitar. Nothing fancy, but it sounded real nice.

"Wow! That's awesome!" Harlie exclaimed. (Harlie is a great guitarist

herself, so I take her opinion seriously.) "That's an acoustic guitar," she told us as it played. "Somebody must have recorded themselves playing the guitar and posted it on your 'Zine."

"But why here?" I wondered. "This section is for the writing contest."

Before anyone could answer, a voice sang out from the computer's speakers. It was a song! Someone had written a song for my contest!

"SShhhhh!" Miss O insisted. "I want to hear it!"

We all leaned in toward the speakers to listen.

"*Are you thinking of me? If I'm not there, do you care?*" the voice sang.

My eyes widened. "Is that—"

Miss O grabbed me. "Juliette! Your poem!"

Harlie turned up the volume on the computer.

"*When I'm not with you I keep wishing I were. Twenty-four-seven, it's always in my brain. But are you doing the same, or to you is this a game?*"

It *was* my poem! Somebody had put it to music!

"Juliette, this is incredible!" Justine gushed. "Your poem sounds so amazing with the music!"

"Who is that singing?" Harlie asked.

My heart was thumping wildly in my chest. "Guys," I said, my voice barely above a whisper, "I think it's *Noah!*"

Chapter 10

Going All "Juliette" on My BFFs

Okay, so I wasn't one-hundred percent sure it was Noah singing the song. But sitting at my computer in my bedroom, after having listened to the song at least twelve more times, I have to say I was ninety-nine point nine percent sure it was him.

I mean, who else could it be?

A. It sounded like him

B. He played guitar

C. He knew I would hear it because I always read my own 'Zine.

D. Lastly, I did some checking from my host computer at home and found out the song was posted by . . . *yes*. . . GreenDayFAN.

Come on! It *had* to be him!

If it *were* Noah, it would certainly explain a lot. Like, for example, why he was waiting for me at my locker this morning. I'm thinking he was probably checking to see if I had listened to the song yet, which I obviously hadn't.

And it would also explain why he'd acted all weird to me in class this morning. Especially if he thought I was ditching Sage Sings to go skiing with Tyler. If I were him, I'd have been weird and distant to me, too.

Anyway, I was practically convinced it was Noah, and I couldn't wait to tell the girls how I'd found out the singer was "GreenDayFan." At the moment, however, they were all still at school. Miss O had indoor soccer practice, Isabella had basketball practice, and Harlie and Justine were doing their homework while waiting for them in the Sage Library. Afterward, they were all walking here together.

I played the song again while I waited. I couldn't help it! I really loved that song. It was a pretty simple melody—just two or three chords over and over again, but it was so sweet. I couldn't believe I was partially responsible for it. That I had written a song . . . with Noah Sclar! A *love* song!

I listened to it three more times before Miss O and the girls finally came home.

"I'm up here!" I called downstairs to them. "Come up quickly! I want to show you something!"

The girls flew up the steps and into my room. They dropped their backpacks on my floor and each found a comfortable place to settle in.

"Did you find a good advice letter to answer?" Miss O asked.

I looked at her. "No! I want to show you something about the *song*," I told her.

"Oh."

"I couldn't get that song—um, *your* song—out of my head all afternoon!" Isabella said excitedly. "I just kept hearing it over and over!"

"And I was whistling it in class," Harlie told us. "But then I got in trouble for whistling," she added.

"Look," I told them. "I found out who posted the song!"

Miss O's eyes widened. "Really?" she asked.

"Who?" Isabella wanted to know.

"GreenDayFAN!" I blurted out.

"Get out!" Justine asked. "The same person from the other letter?"

I nodded. "*Noah Sclar*," I corrected her. "I'm positive it's him!" I ran through my alphabetized list of reasons for them. "And 'E,'" I added, "he knows I love Green Day because of that time at my locker when my cell phone rang."

"That's true," Harlie commented.

"Boy, Juliette! This is so cool!" Miss O said with a romantic sigh. "Aren't you stoked? I mean, it's pretty obvious that Noah likes you."

"Yeah! Like, what are you going to say to him tomorrow morning at school?" Isabella asked.

I shrugged. "I don't know," I answered. "Well, I'll probably tell him I really love the song."

"Oooh! Let's see if anybody else has heard the song yet!" Justine said excitedly.

"Okay, Jus," I said, turning back to my computer screen. "Let me refresh the screen and see if there are more comments."

The girls all crowded around me as the computer refreshed. When we saw the number of comments next to the song posting had hit fifty, we all freaked out.

"Holy moley!" Harlie cried. "That's just from today! Come on, Juliette! Click on some to see what they say!"

Together we read the new comments. Every single one of them was about the song.

My song.

Mine and Noah's song!

COMMENTS: TOTALLY THE BOMB, DUDE! AWESOME SONG! WHO R U ANYWAY?

COMMENTS: BEST SONG EVER! WHO WROTE THE MUSIC?

COMMENTS: WHO IS SINGING THIS? DO WE KNOW YOU? GREAT SONG, BTW.

COMMENTS: WHO IS SINGING THIS SONG? JULIETTE, DO YOU KNOW WHO IT IS?

Nearly everybody wanted to know who the singer was. They already knew it was me who wrote the poem, but now the big mystery was:

Who wrote the music? Everyone wanted me to tell them who it was! But I couldn't tell them it was Noah. He would have to reveal that himself.

I must have been totally lost in thought because Miss O threw a pillow at me.

"Juliette? Hello? I just asked you something!"

"Huh? Sorry! What?" I mumbled.

"I asked you how you were going to finish the new issue of the 'Zine? There's still so much more to do, and you have a tennis match tonight. Then we're leaving for Windham right after school tomorrow."

I groaned. "Don't remind me!" I said. "I still can't believe we're missing Sage Sings."

"Let's not talk about that anymore. Let's just finish the 'Zine because the girls can't stay long today."

"Yeah, sorry I can't stay too long, Juliette," Justine said. "I have to be home for dinner tonight."

"Me, too," Isabella said. "I have so much homework to do."

I felt a little panicky. "I thought you just did your homework!" I said to Isabella.

"Well, I still have more," she replied.

"And I have a lot to do tonight, too," Miss O chimed in. "Plus I have to pack for the trip."

I took a deep breath. "Then we'd *really* better get started right now!" I told them all.

"So, what first?" Harlie asked. "Will your dad help me scan my comic strip into the computer? It's practically finished and—"

"Harlie!" I cried out in alarm. "It's not finished yet?"

"Well, it's *almost* finished!" Harlie replied. "I haven't had time to—"

"Well, now what am I going to do?" I blurted out in a panic. "You have to finish it right now!" I urged. "So my father can scan it in when he gets home!"

"But . . . but I don't have my colored pencils," Harlie protested.

"Oh, great!" I muttered in frustration. "Well, then let's make sure everything *else* is typed into the computer right now. Then on Sunday, after we get back from skiing, I guess I can just finish posting it all. Justine, do you have your interviews?"

Justine stared at the floor. "Well, I couldn't interview all six kids this time. I only managed to do four."

"Oh, no!" I cried. "Really? Your article isn't done yet either?"

Justine sighed. "No. Sorry, Juliette. But I didn't have enough time—"

I was feeling so angry at my friends, I didn't know what to do! How could they do this to me? Didn't they know how important this 'Zine was to me?

I tried to take a deep breath and calm down. Getting angrier at them was not going to make my 'Zine appear any faster.

"Okay. Never mind," I said. "What do you have so far?" I asked Justine.

Justine pulled open her messenger bag and took out a notebook. "Well, I interviewed kids for their opinions on what they thought the Sage School needed most," she explained.

"Really?" Harlie asked. "What did they say?"

Justine read aloud from her notebook. "Okay. One kid said we needed a game room," she said.

We all laughed.

"Can you imagine?" Harlie asked. "How cool would that be?"

"You would never get any work done!" I told her. "We would find you in there playing *Crime Fighter* every day!"

Harlie grinned. "True," she said with a giggle. "I love that game."

"Ooooh, and what if they had *Dance, Dance Revolution?*" Miss O added. "Me and Juliette would probably miss lunch every day to play that!"

"Okay, okay. Come on, guys! Let's just get back to this!" I pleaded with the girls.

"Um, sorry, Juliette," Justine murmured. She checked her notebook again. "And this one," she said, "is from a kid in middle division. She said she thinks Sage School needs a coffee bar."

"Amen to that!" Harlie joked. The girls all laughed. It was common knowledge that Harlie adored mocha lattes.

"And this one is so funny," Justine went on. "From this kid in upper division. He said he thinks Sage School really needs a pool!"

"Huh?" I asked. "But we *have* a pool!"

Justine laughed. "I know! I told him that, and he said, 'Really?' I mean, he's been at our school for how many years, and he didn't know we had a pool?"

"Some people are just clueless!" Harlie said with a laugh.

The girls began talking about the dopey kid from upper division and I couldn't believe they were acting so calm about my project. As if everything were just peachy, and that I wasn't completely stressing over getting it all done.

"Is that all?" I asked Justine.

The girls stopped chatting. Justine nodded.

"Okay. So maybe you can start typing in your interviews right now. Then we can hook your camera into my computer and download the pictures of these kids."

"Sure," Justine said, taking my seat at the computer.

I pressed my fingers into my temples to help me think. Okay, what next? My tennis match would take two hours. Then I would have to shower, finish my homework, and scan all that stuff into the computer with Dad.

Oh, brother. How was I going to do all that? There weren't enough hours left in the day for me to finish everything! Even with my friends helping, there was no way it could all get done tonight.

My heart started racing as I thought about how disappointed Mr. Adams would be if my 'Zine failed. Not to mention, I'd be the joke of my Computer Clicks class. The joke of the school! I couldn't let this project fall flat. I just couldn't!

But how was I going to prepare the entire next issue . . . in just a few hours?

"Type faster, Justine!" I instructed.

"Sir, yes, sir!" Justine replied instinctively. "Oh. Uh, sorry, Juliette. I'm just used to answering that way when I'm given orders. You know, with my father being a general and all."

"Isabella, what about you?" I asked. "Can you have dinner here tonight and help type some stuff?"

"No, sorry Juliette," Isabella replied. "My parents want me home for dinner tonight. But, I guess I can take some work home to do. Um, if you want me to, that is."

"Okay," I told her. "Good idea. You can type your sports article into the computer tonight at home. Save it on a disc and bring the disc here tomorrow morning before we walk to school."

"Uh, how do I do that?" Isabella asked.

"You mean you don't know how to save stuff on a disc?" I asked in amazement.

"I'm not the one who has Computer Clicks, *chica*," Isabella said in annoyance. "I don't know how to do anything on the computer except IM! So shoot me!"

I sighed. "Well, then, just IM me tonight when you have it all typed in and I'll walk you through it," I replied.

"What's left?" Miss O asked. "Did you read through the new advice problems?"

I groaned. "Why do you keep asking me that?" I asked her. "That's the only part of the 'Zine that's ready to go! That, and my blog. All finished! I just need the stuff from you guys!"

"Well, Juliette," Miss O insisted, "You can't expect us all to drop everything else and stop our lives for *your* school project!"

The room grew quiet.

"I know that," I said.

"Well you need to just take a chill pill and relax!" my sister went on. "We're helping you the best we can. You can be a little more appreciative, and a little nicer! We're tired of being bossed—that's all I'm saying!"

I ran my fingers through my hair in frustration. "Well you can also be a little more understanding of what I'm going through!" I shot back.

Harlie stood in between us and held up her hand.

"Time out!" she cried. "Time out, sisters! We need to stop arguing, or nothing is going to get done."

I nodded. "You're right," I said with a sigh. "I'm sorry. I'm just really frazzled here and I'm taking it out on you guys. Sorry."

What was happening to me? I wondered. When had I become so nuts?

I gasped, slowly realizing what was going on.

I had gone all "Juliette" on my BFFs!

Chapter 11

Almost Famous

My mom always talks about what it was like when she went to college. (Actually, that's where she met my dad, at college. They both lived in the same dormitory.) Mom says she had tons of work in college, and sometimes she would have to stay up all night to finish it. Then she would always make a joke about having to put toothpicks in her eyes to help keep them open the next day, so she wouldn't fall asleep in class!

I always thought that joke was way gross, but after staying up so, so late last night, this morning I was thinking, "Hey! I could really use some toothpicks!"

Anyway, thanks to my extremely helpful little sister (I think we both were feeling pretty badly about what had happened yesterday after school), I was now dressed and ready to go, even though I had slept through my alarm clock. Miss O had picked out an outfit for me, made me breakfast,

and put together my book bag for school. (Best Sister Ever Award definitely goes to her.)

Isabella had come through for me, too, and brought over the disc with her sports article, which we had just loaded onto my computer. My long, long list of responsibilities was now a teensy bit shorter, and the new issue of Sage 'Zine Zcene would be all ready to post on the Web Sunday night when we got back from skiing.

Hopefully.

As we walked to school, we were talking about the song (again!) when I felt my bag buzz. I reached inside and pulled out my cell phone, which, just so you know, now played "my song" when it rang.

"You already made the song your new ring tone?" Isabella asked as we walked.

I nodded and flipped open the phone.

"Cool," she muttered.

"It's a text," I told the girls. "But I'm not sure who it's from." We all stopped walking to read the message.

CAN U MEET ME B4 CLASS AT UR LOCKER? – NOAH

"Omigod! Noah is text-messaging you?" Miss O cried. "Wow!"

I felt a shiver run down my spine. It was Noah all right! I couldn't believe it. When I gave him my cell number last week, I never thought he'd actually use it.

"Come on," I said to the girls. "I have to get to my locker right away! Let's pick up the pace!"

Miss O laughed. "I never saw you in such a rush to get to school before!" she said.

"Well that's because I've never been text-messaged by a cute guy before," I replied. "Come on! You guys are moving too slow!"

I waited by my locker for Noah, and when he didn't show up, I started to think that maybe it hadn't really been him who sent that text. Maybe it had been a joke?

If that were true, I was going to be way mad!

Thankfully, two minutes before the bell for class, I saw Noah heading toward me.

"Did you get my text?" Noah asked.

I nodded. "Yeah, what's up?" I asked him.

"We should head to class," he said. "I didn't realize I would be late."

"Okay, let's walk," I said, secretly excited for everyone to see me walking to class with Noah Sclar.

"Did you happen to see your 'Zine yesterday?" Noah asked me.

I laughed. "Of course I did! I check it, like, ten times a day!" I told him.

"Right. Dumb question," he said. "But anyway, I wanted to ask you about the song—" he started to say.

Unfortunately, Noah didn't get a chance to finish. Just as we approached our classroom, we found Tyler Brooks waiting by the door.

"Uh, hey, can I talk to you for a second?" Tyler asked.

Was this really happening? I wondered. Was Tyler totally ruining my "moment" with Noah? I felt like screaming, *Not now, Tyler! Can't you see Noah was just about to tell me he wrote that song just for me? Because he has a*

huge crush on me and is so, so bummed I won't be able to go to Sage Sings? Can't you see that???

Instead, I stopped myself from saying anything. After all, I had already been obnoxious to Tyler twice this week and I was still feeling pretty bad about it. I didn't want him to think I was a Class A Witch, after all. "Uh, okay, Tyler. What's up?"

"It's, um, well, it's about snowboarding."

Just then, Mr. Adams walked past us and into the classroom. "Let's find our seats, students," he said. "We have a lot to do today."

I shot an apologetic look at Tyler. Whatever his "snowboarding emergency" was, it was going to have to wait.

"I really have to go," I told him.

Tyler nodded. "Yeah, okay," he said. "No problem. I guess I'll see you later then," he said. He headed down the hallway and I stepped into my classroom.

I quickly took my seat next to Noah and whispered to him as Mr. Adams took attendance. "Sorry about that!" I said. "What did you want to ask me?"

"It's about your song," Noah whispered back.

My heart leapt. But didn't he mean "our" song? I wondered.

"What about it?" I asked.

"Well, I know there's not a lot of time," Noah whispered. "But I really wanted to play it at Sage Sings, if the band could learn it by then."

"Really?" I asked in surprise. "You want to sing it at Sage Sings? That's awesome!"

"Everybody is talking about it," Noah said. "It's a pretty decent song. That's why I text-messaged you this morning from my friend's cell. Everybody on the bus was talking about the song, and I thought it would be cool for As If to learn it in time for the concert tomorrow night. Well, I mean, if you said it was okay."

"Yeah, I mean, sure!" I said. "But you don't have to ask me—" I started to say. That's when Mr. Adams cleared his throat, which I knew meant "stop talking and pay attention."

I sat back in my seat and only half-listened to Mr. Adams talk about a new piece of computer equipment we'd just received in class. I couldn't concentrate—so much was happening! People were talking about my song! I really *was* almost famous! And Noah wanted to perform the song in front of the whole school. How romantic was that?

And how completely devastated was I that I wouldn't be there to hear it?

Normally, I would be psyched to get picked up early from school for the purpose of going on vacation. But today, I was anything *but*. I'd been looking forward to lunchtime all morning, so I could talk more to Noah about the song and Sage Sings. I mean, this was *my day*! The day everyone would learn it was Noah who had put my words to music and created the most awesome song ever.

But my parents had to go and ruin it by surprising me with an early pickup.

When I first heard the intercom buzz in French class, I had no idea it was about me. But then I heard my French teacher call my name.

"Juliette," she said. *"ton père t'attend, prends tes affaires et va au bureau. Tu vas rentrer à la maison maintenant."*

It took me a moment to translate in my head what Madame Kirshner had just said. I was supposed to take my things and head to the office to meet my father, who was waiting to pick me up, but all I could hope for was that she'd gotten the message wrong. That my father wasn't picking me up early. I didn't want to leave just yet!

I paid a visit to my locker and collected what I would need for the week-end (not much). Then I headed to the office, where I found Dad and Miss O waiting for me.

"We're leaving early!" Miss O said excitedly.

I ignored her. "Dad, do we have to leave now?" I asked.

Dad was at the front desk, signing me out. "Yes," he said. "Your mother and I have already packed the car," he told me. "We decided to treat you girls and take you out early."

"But I don't want to leave yet," I protested. "Please? Can't you pick me up later? Like, after lunch?"

"Juliette! What's the problem?" Miss O asked. "Aren't you psyched? We get a half-day!"

"No! I really want to stay for lunch!" I told them both. *And talk to Noah more about our song,* I added in my head.

"Sorry, sweetie," Dad said. I followed him out of the office, then out of the school.

"But, Dad! This isn't fair!" I insisted.

"Juliette, you're nuts!" Miss O said. "Would you be quiet? I want to leave! I don't want to go back to class!"

I made a face at her. "But Noah—" I began in a whisper.

Miss O rolled her eyes. "Get past it, Juliette!" she whispered back. "Forget about Noah, and the song, and Sage Sings. We're going skiing! Just forget about all that other stuff and get psyched for our trip already!"

"Hi, Hon!" Mom called to me from the car. She was beaming. "Ready to hit the slopes?"

I didn't talk to anyone for the entire ride home. And then, for the whole car trip upstate. Even though we had a walkie talkies thing going on with Tyler's car as we caravanned to Windham, I refused to join in the fun.

I was mad—and I felt like being mad! So I just turned up the volume on my iPod and stared out the window as we drove north.

This was going to be the worst vacation of my life.

Chapter 12

From Bored to Board

I knew Miss O was angry at me for being such a pouty-pants. But I couldn't help it. I was still so mad that we had left school early, and that I was missing Sage Sings this weekend. How come nobody ever asked me what I wanted to do?

When we arrived at Moose Lodge, Miss O convinced my parents to let us go in the hot tub on the deck off our room. I have admit I *was* kind of excited to do that, since it was so cold out. I'd never been in an outdoor hot tub in the winter before!

We put on our bathing suits and went next door to get Dana and Tyler. Minutes later, the four of us were hanging out in the hot, hot water on the deck, looking at the snowy mountains around us.

I confess . . . it was pretty cool.

As we simmered, I heard Tyler mention that he had his laptop computer with him for the weekend.

"No way, really?" I asked.

Tyler nodded.

I gazed excitedly at Miss O. "Do you know what this means?" I asked her.

My sister's eyes widened. "No, what?" she asked.

"We can work on finishing the 'Zine!" I exclaimed. "I brought the disc just in case. And since Tyler has his laptop I can get it altogether and you can type in your recipe and then proofread—"

"*Whoa!*" Miss O cried, holding a hand up out of the steamy water. "I am *not* doing schoolwork this weekend!"

I blinked at her in confusion. "But it's not schoolwork!" I insisted. "It's my 'Zine!"

"That's right! It's *your* 'Zine!" Miss O repeated. "So if you want to do any work on your ski vacation, be my guest! I am off-duty!"

"I can help you," Tyler offered meekly.

"Thank you, Tyler!" I said loud enough for Miss O to get the gist of how mad at her I was. "Thanks for offering! You're a real friend!"

I sat back and felt my blood boil. I don't know if it was because I was boiling mad at my sister, or because I was sitting in boiling hot water.

Even Dana suggesting we play Twenty Questions couldn't cheer me up. (And Miss O and I usually rocked at that game.)

"Are you young or old?" Tyler asked me.

"Old, I guess," I replied.

"Are you on television?" Dana asked.

I nodded. "That's five," I said.

"Do you have gray hair?" Miss O asked.

"No. I'm older, but not that old," I said. "That's question number six."

"Are you Uncle Steven?" Tyler asked.

We all burst out laughing. "Your Uncle Steven is on television?" I asked in between laughs.

Tyler's face turned red. "No! I don't know why I said that!" he cried. "My Uncle Steven just popped into my head—I forgot that you said the person was on television."

"Oh! Are you on a reality show?" Miss O asked.

I nodded again.

"Are you Jeff Probst from *Survivor*?" Miss O cried.

"Yes!"

"Drat!" Tyler joked. "I was so sure it was Uncle Steven."

We all laughed.

Okay, I was starting to feel *slightly* better.

That night, our parents brought pizza in to the room. It was brick oven pizza, which is my all-time favorite kind of pizza because I like crispy crusts. After dinner, we went downstairs to the teen hangout where they were showing an Adam Sandler movie.

I'll admit it.

I was having fun. I, too, wanted nothing to do with working on the 'Zine on vacation. And after dinner I realized I'd gone a whole hour without thinking about Noah or Sage Sings *once*.

The next morning, we were up and out on the mountain early. Miss O, Dana, and I picked up our snowboarding rental equipment and followed Tyler to the snowboarding instructional spot at the bottom of the mountain. It was a beautiful winter day—cold, but not freezing or windy—and I couldn't wait to try snowboarding. I was wearing my new bright blue ski suit, and Dad had bought both Miss O and me our own helmets and goggles. I have to say, we both looked pretty fab!

Tyler was being so funny! And an excellent instructor, too! He didn't laugh once when I messed up, except for the time when I fell on my butt and then Miss O fell on top of me. But we all laughed because Miss O yelled out, "Duck!" right before she fell on me, and we couldn't figure out why she'd said, "Duck."

Tyler helped us up. "Duck?" he asked my sister.

Miss O's cheeks were already red from the cold, but I could tell she was blushing. "I don't know! I couldn't think of anything else to say!"

I got up and brushed the snow off of me.

"Duck?" I asked her. "Are you insane? How about, 'Watch out'? or 'Coming through'?"

"Sorry, Juliette," Miss O said. "That's just what came out. Are you okay?"

"Yeah, I'm fine," I told her. Then I turned to Tyler. "So what do you say, teach? Are we ready for the lift?"

"Definitely," Tyler said. "Let's head over to the D Lift. We'll start on an easy one." He grabbed his snowboard and pulled his goggles down over his eyes. He was wearing a bright blue ski suit, too, and one of those crazy, multicolored ski hats that had pointy pieces going in all directions and looked like a court jester's hat.

You know what?

He looked really cute decked out in ski clothes.

When we got to the chairlift, I rode up with Dana, and Miss O took a lift with Tyler.

"This is so much fun," Dana said.

"Yeah, it is," I replied.

"Can I tell you something?" Dana asked me.

I nodded. "Sure. What's up?" I asked.

"Well, I have you to thank for me and Tyler getting along better," she said.

"How come?" I asked.

"Well, last week Tyler and I had it out," she went on. "He told me he thought I was treating him badly and that he wanted us to be friends, and I started to realize that I had been pretty mean to him lately."

"Wow."

"He told me that you gave him the advice to talk to me," she added.

I thought about it, and then nodded. "I did," I said. "I guess my advice really does work!" I added with a laugh.

"Yup. So we made up," she said. "And now we're cool."

"Great!" I told her.

Just then, from behind us we heard a voice echo loudly.

"*Duck!*"

We spun around in our seat to see Miss O and Tyler in the chairlift behind us. They were cracking up.

"You're pathetic!" I called back to my sister. Then I faced forward and prepared to get off the lift. That was the hardest part about snowboarding, I thought—getting off the chairlift! It was tricky, and if you didn't get it just

right, you could fall. Or, you could panic and not get off the lift at all, which is exactly what happened to Miss O!

"*Juje!*" she cried, as her chair swung around the turn to head back down the mountain.

"Why didn't you jump off?" I called up to her.

She put up her hands and shrugged. "I forgot!" she called back.

I exchanged looks with Dana and Tyler. Then, at the same time, we all called up to her as she traveled back down the mountain with the other empty chair lifts.

"Duck!" we all yelled together.

Then we burst into laughter.

That night, I rested my sore legs on the comfy chairs in the Moose Lodge lounge and sipped the tastiest cup of cocoa in New York. I was wearing my favorite après-ski outfit: flannel bottoms, an extra large sweatshirt that said "Sage," and gym socks with my Adidas flip-flops. I took a sip of my cocoa, swallowed slowly, then snuggled deeper into my lounge chair.

"This is the best!" I sighed.

"Tell me about it," Miss O said. "I love these chairs facing the mountain. How pretty does that look?"

We watched the night skiers as they sped down the mountain under the lights. It was beautiful.

"I wish we could live at Moose Lodge all the time," Dana chimed in. "This is so much fun. I'm not even upset anymore about missing Sage Sings."

Miss O and I exchanged looks. Mainly because, I guess, we were both surprised at how neither of us had even mentioned Sage Sings all day! How weird is that? Yesterday I was completely miserable because I couldn't go, and now I had forgotten all about it!

"Can I ask you something?" I said to Miss O as we sipped.

"Sure! What's up?" she asked.

"It's about the 'Zine," I started to say.

"Ugh, Juliette!" she replied instantly. "Please! Off-duty . . . remember?"

"Yes! I know, I know!" I replied. "It's not about that. About work, I mean."

Miss O sighed. "Then what?" she asked.

"Are you 'Tired of Being Bossed'?" I asked her.

Miss O looked at me. "When did you figure it out?" she asked.

"Believe it or not, just today," I told her. "I was talking to Dana earlier, and she said that the advice I gave to Tyler really worked. That got me thinking about the other advice I'd given, and that's when it hit me. That letter was from you."

Miss O nodded.

"I've been horrible, haven't I?" I asked glumly.

Miss O laughed. "No. Not horrible," she replied. "You just got all . . . all . . ."

"All Juliette, right?"

We both laughed. "Yeah. All Juliette," she said.

"I'm really sorry, Miss O," I said. "You'll be happy to know I'm going to chill out over the whole 'Zine thing, too," I told her.

"Yeah?" she asked.

I nodded. "Yup. I mean, I was just seeing how great it was all day

today, to just relax and have fun and not worry about the 'Zine. It's been awesome!"

"Yeah, it has," she agreed.

"So I've decided to do the 'Zine once a month, instead of once a week," I told her.

"Excellent idea!" my sister said.

"Yeah, Tyler really gave *me* some good advice," I told her. "When we were on top of the mountain this afternoon, about to come down on our boards, Tyler said to me, 'Just remember to stop and smell the snow.'"

"Huh?" Miss O asked. "Isn't it, 'Stop and smell the roses'?" she asked.

"Yeah, but I knew what he meant," I explained. "I've got to take things easier. Relax more. Remember to have fun. It's easy to get all caught up in something and forget why you're doing it in the first place. That was what happened to me," I added. "I kind of got caught in the 'Net!"

"Ha," Miss O said.

"Where is Tyler anyway?" I asked Dana.

Dana shrugged. "I'm not sure. I think he was coming downstairs with our parents."

"You seem kind of into Tyler today, Juliette," Miss O commented. "Are you crushing?"

My eyes widened and I kicked my sister in the leg. "No way! What is your problem?"

Dana sat upright in her chair. "Do you like my brother?" she asked. "That would be so excellent!" she cried. "Do you?"

"No! Both of you, just drop it! You're crazy!" But I felt my cheeks turn red. Why was I blushing?

Were they right?

Was I crushing on Tyler Brooks?

Just then, Mom, Dad, Tyler, and his parents came into the lounge. We'd found seats for all of us near the big picture window next to the fireplace. It was really, I thought, the coziest spot on the planet!

"Hey!" Dad said as they joined us. "We brought our guitars. Feel like hearing some music?"

"Yes!" we all said excitedly. Dad and Mr. Brooks always played guitars together. They were so good—they sometimes even played songs that we liked.

Tyler sat down across from me, and I don't know why, but my cheeks got hot when he grinned at me. He *did* look pretty cute in his Sage flannels and sweatshirt. And his hair had that messy, just-shampooed look.

To my surprise, Tyler had a guitar with him, too. I didn't even know he played.

Dad and Tyler's father began to play a bunch of Beatles songs that we all knew. It was so fun! I loved singing along while my father played the guitar. It was one of my most favorite things to do. Pretty soon, other people in the lounge came over and joined our little "concert." I have to tell you, it was like we were having our own little Sage Sings!

We finished singing my favorite Beatles song of all time, "In My Life," (that song always makes me and Miss O cry!) when Tyler picked up his guitar.

"I didn't know you played," I said.

Tyler nodded.

"What kind of music do you play?" I asked.

"Lots of stuff," Tyler replied. "Beatles, Green Day . . . "

"I love Green Day!" I cried. "Can you play something by them?"

"Tyler is an excellent guitarist," my father chimed in. "I keep telling him we want him in our rock band!"

Tyler made a face, and I laughed. "Well, I do like jamming with you and my dad. But unless you play more songs that were written *after* 1975, then I'll pass!"

We giggled. "Come on, play something, Tyler," I said. I was really seeing a whole other side to Tyler Brooks today. He hadn't been shy or awkward or uncomfortable once.

"Okay," Tyler said finally. "I have a new song to play."

I leaned back in my chair and watched as he began to strum the guitar strings. I lifted my mug of cocoa toward my lips and started to take a sip, when the chords Tyler was playing began to sound familiar. I lowered my mug and stared at him in shock.

Tyler was playing *my song*!

Miss O, Dana, and I sat upright in our chairs. As Tyler sang, his voice was incredible. He knew the words by heart and he played the chords exactly like they were played on the sound clip I'd listened to a hundred times in my room.

It was my song. Mine and Noah's song, but I was beginning to realize that Noah Sclar indeed had nothing to do with the song after all.

Tyler glanced my way as he played, and all at once I knew.

He was the mysterious singer.

Chapter 13

Taking My Own Advice

How could I have not seen that?

How could I have been so wrong?

Everything began to make sense suddenly. I had been all wrong about Noah. He wasn't into me. He didn't put my poem to music. In fact, the more I thought about it, I wasn't entirely sure Noah had ever even read my 'Zine!

It had been Tyler all along. And I had been so caught up in thinking Noah liked me, I couldn't see that Tyler was actually more my type. It's true: we liked the same music, the same television shows, we both loved to write . . . all the things I had thought Noah and I had in common, it was actually Tyler and me instead.

Boy, had I made a mistake.

"Tyler, I really love what you did with my poem," I told him when he'd finished singing, and the "audience" that had gathered around our families had finished applauding.

"I wasn't sure you had heard the clip," he said.

"The whole school heard the clip!" Miss O butted in. "That's, like, the most popular song at school right now!"

"Noah Sclar asked me if As If could play it tonight at Sage Sings," I told Tyler. I noticed his expression changed when I mentioned Noah.

"I told him yes," I said. "And I was actually pretty bummed I wouldn't be there tonight to hear it."

Tyler lowered his head and nodded. "Yeah, I know you were upset about coming to Windham this weekend and missing Sage Sings."

"I was," I admitted. "But only because I wouldn't get to hear the song. And you know what? Hearing it here, tonight, was way better!"

Tyler looked up at me. "Yeah?" he asked.

"Definitely," I said.

"Wanna hear another song I wrote?" he asked.

"Yes!" I said excitedly. I settled back in my comfy chair and sipped a little more cocoa.

I couldn't believe what an excellent day this had turned out to be. And to think I had begged and pleaded with my parents not to come! Boy was I happy they'd insisted.

Best of all, I had learned something about myself—as dorky as that sounds. It's kind of like that old saying, "Don't judge a book by its cover." I had formed an opinion about Tyler based on an impression. And I had let people at school change the way I thought about him.

But now, I knew that nothing was ever as it seemed. I mean, who would have thought that shy, awkward Tyler Brooks could be such an adorable musician? If you had told me that last week, I would have said you were nuts.

And now, here he was, about to play me another song he'd written. It was probably another love song, something sweet and beautiful, and romantic like *our* song. Isn't it funny how some things turn out?

I closed my eyes and let the fire warm my face. I prepared to get lost in the romance of his music.

"This song is about my favorite video game, *Star Fire*," Tyler explained as he began to strum the guitar. "And how this one intergalactic alien comes to Earth and—"

Oh, well, I thought, laughing quietly to myself. *Some things, I guess, are as they seem!*